UNCLE SILAS

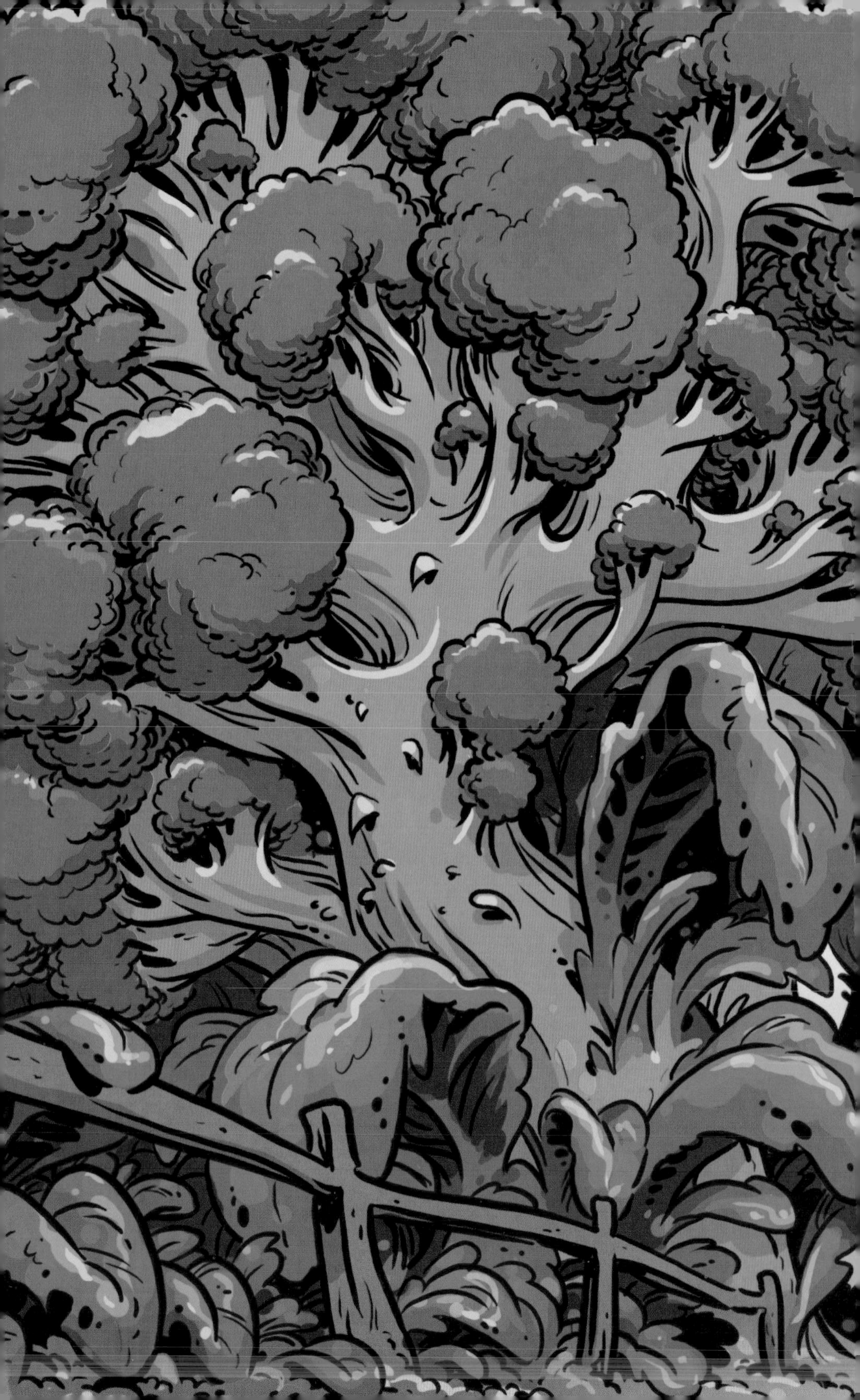

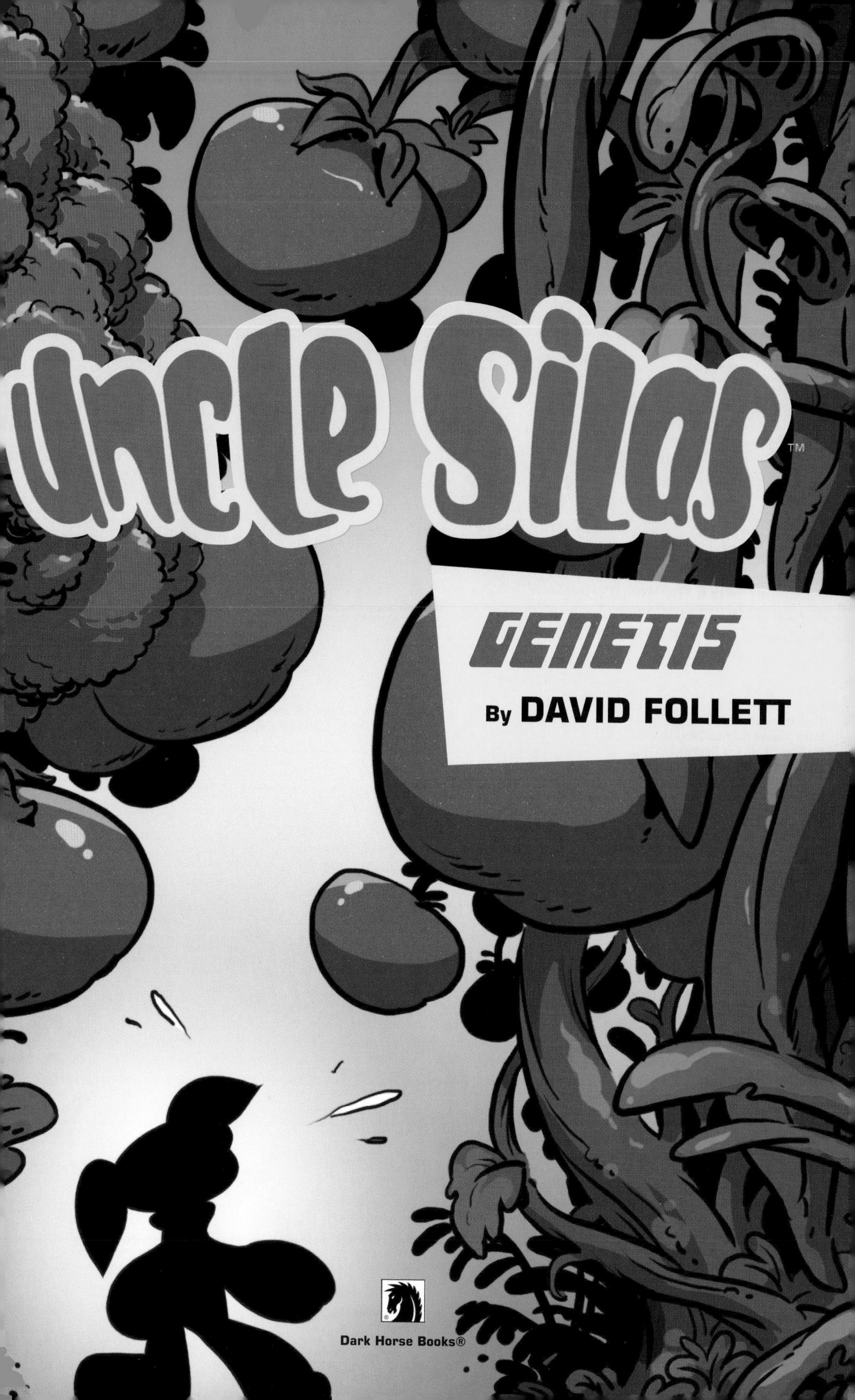

Uncle Silas™

Genetis

By DAVID FOLLETT

Dark Horse Books®

Publisher MIKE RICHARDSON
Editor DAVE MARSHALL
Assistant Editor BRENDAN WRIGHT
Designer TONY ONG

Published by
Dark Horse Books
A division of
Dark Horse Comics, Inc.
10956 SE Main Street
Milwaukie, OR 97222

darkhorse.com

Library of Congress Cataloging-in-Publication Data

Follett, David.
  Uncle Silas : genetis / by David Follett. -- 1st ed.
    p. cm.
  ISBN 978-1-59582-566-7
  1. Graphic novels. I. Title.
  PN6790.A83F65 2010
  741.5'973--dc22
                              2010014584

First edition: October 2010

10 9 8 7 6 5 4 3 2 1
Printed by Midas Printing International, Ltd.,
Huizhou, China.

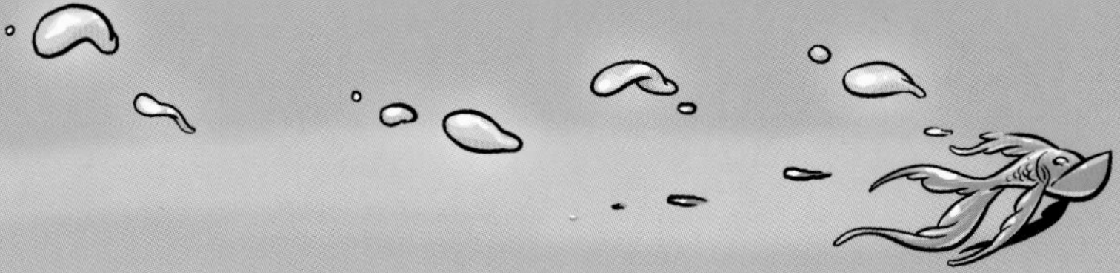

For Robin, Jim, and Dayna.

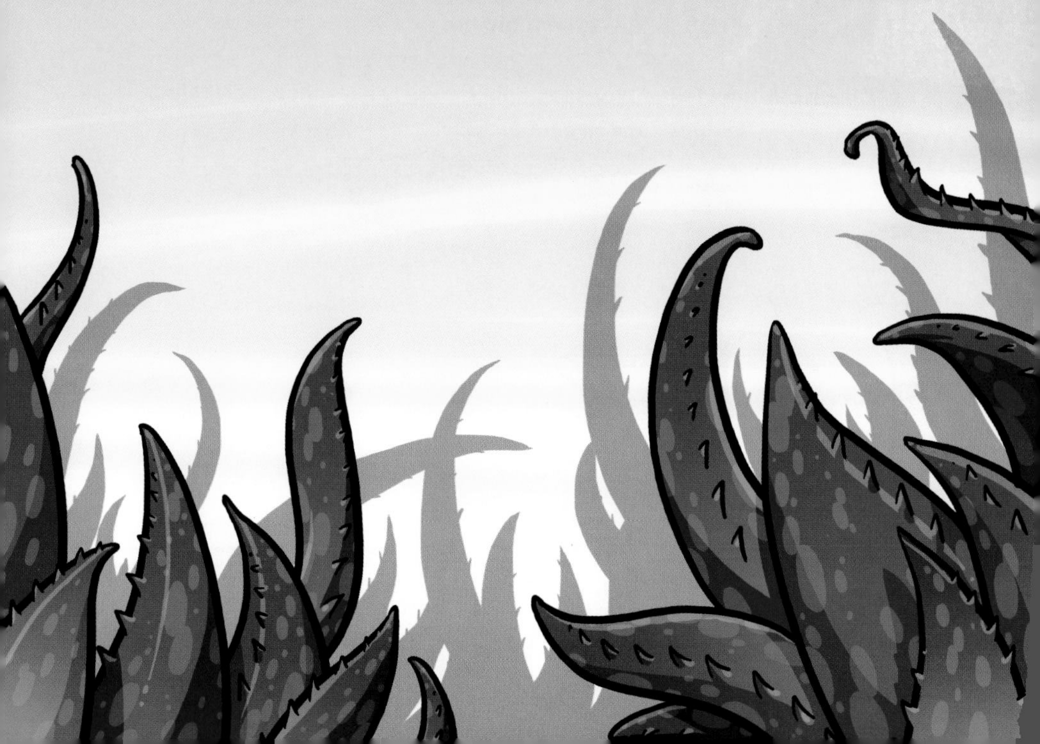

THANKS TO ALL THOSE ALONG THE WAY WHO HELPED! Pat for asking eight-plus years ago, "Got any ideas for a Sunday newspaper comic strip?" To Mo, Tom J., Eloise, Charlie, and all the other News crew who supported it. To Phill for the verbal abuse and camaraderie in the studio. Hope I gave as good as I got. To Shaun for legal advice. Massive thanks to Tom Brown and Tony Giles for their help coloring the flats for me; you guys saved me months of time and my sanity! Couldn't have met the deadline without you two.

Thanks also to my family for their support and lerv. Jim especially, for being the inspiration for Uncle Silas, and Dayna for Selena. This was meant to be something you'd be reading when you were twelve years old, Dayna—I'm sorry for the wait! Thanks also to all those at DH who have helped make this happen! Biggest thanks of all to Christie for her patience while I worked on this outside of work hours and on weekends for four-plus years. I look back, count up the hours it's taken me, and agree with you all—I am a bit crazy.

Check out unclesilas.blogspot.com for early sketches, scribbles, character designs, and promo artwork.

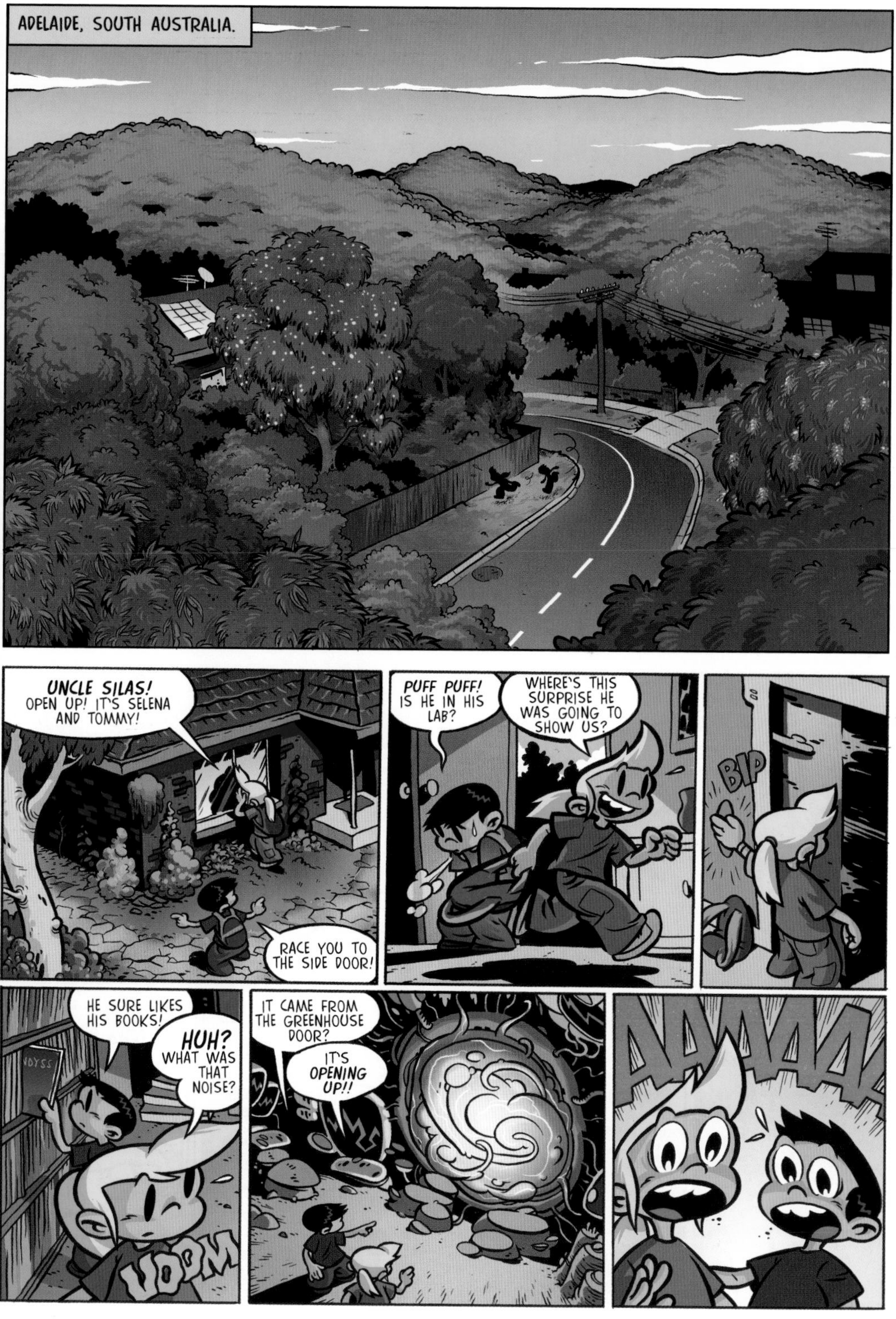

ADELAIDE, SOUTH AUSTRALIA.
UNCLE SILAS! OPEN UP! IT'S SELENA AND TOMMY!
RACE YOU TO THE SIDE DOOR!
PUFF PUFF! IS HE IN HIS LAB?
WHERE'S THIS SURPRISE HE WAS GOING TO SHOW US?
BIP
HE SURE LIKES HIS BOOKS!
HUH? WHAT WAS THAT NOISE?
VOOM
IT CAME FROM THE GREENHOUSE DOOR?
IT'S OPENING UP!!
AAAAA

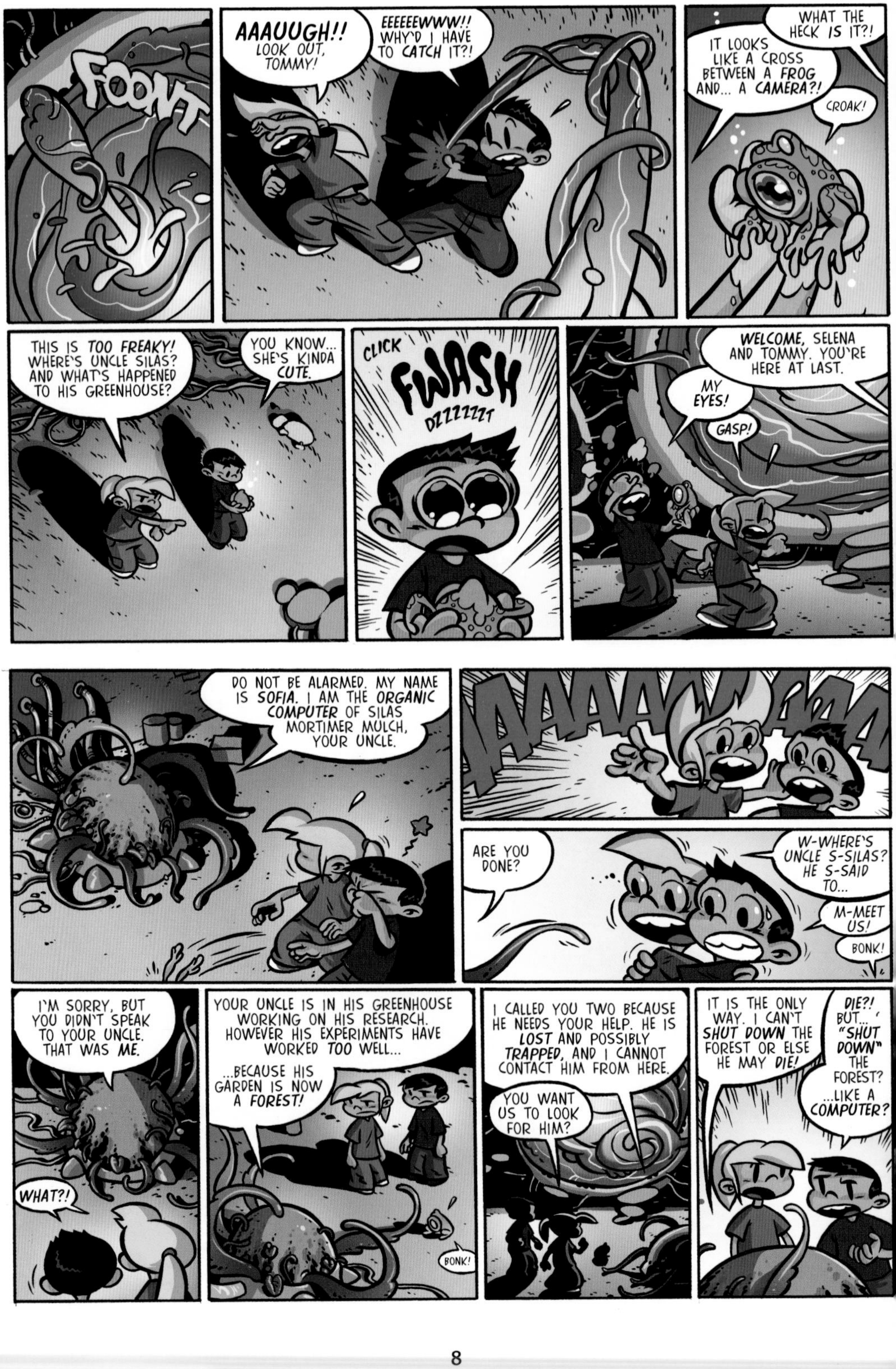
FOONT
AAAUUGH!! LOOK OUT, TOMMY!
EEEEEEWWW!! WHY'D I HAVE TO CATCH IT?!
WHAT THE HECK IS IT?!
IT LOOKS LIKE A CROSS BETWEEN A FROG AND... A CAMERA?!
CROAK!
THIS IS TOO FREAKY! WHERE'S UNCLE SILAS? AND WHAT'S HAPPENED TO HIS GREENHOUSE?
YOU KNOW... SHE'S KINDA CUTE.
CLICK
FWASH
DZZZZZZT
WELCOME, SELENA AND TOMMY. YOU'RE HERE AT LAST.
MY EYES!
GASP!
DO NOT BE ALARMED. MY NAME IS SOFIA. I AM THE ORGANIC COMPUTER OF SILAS MORTIMER MULCH, YOUR UNCLE.
ARE YOU DONE?
W-WHERE'S UNCLE S-SILAS? HE S-SAID TO...
M-MEET US!
BONK!
I'M SORRY, BUT YOU DIDN'T SPEAK TO YOUR UNCLE. THAT WAS ME.
WHAT?!
YOUR UNCLE IS IN HIS GREENHOUSE WORKING ON HIS RESEARCH. HOWEVER HIS EXPERIMENTS HAVE WORKED TOO WELL...
...BECAUSE HIS GARDEN IS NOW A FOREST!
BONK!
I CALLED YOU TWO BECAUSE HE NEEDS YOUR HELP. HE IS LOST AND POSSIBLY TRAPPED, AND I CANNOT CONTACT HIM FROM HERE.
YOU WANT US TO LOOK FOR HIM?
IT IS THE ONLY WAY. I CAN'T SHUT DOWN THE FOREST OR ELSE HE MAY DIE!
DIE?! BUT... "SHUT DOWN" THE FOREST? ...LIKE A COMPUTER?

LET ME EXPLAIN YOUR UNCLE'S WORK: TREES AND PLANTS CURRENTLY HAVE *NO DEFENSE* AGAINST HUMANS... BUT AFTER *YEARS* OF TESTING, SILAS HAS FINALLY FOUND A WAY TO HELP FLORA *SURVIVE.*

OBSERVE...

BAMF

BY SPLICING PLANT PROTEIN CHAINS WITH *ELECTROMETERS* AND *ORGANIC NANOTECHNOLOGY,* YOUR UNCLE HAS SPED UP THE REGROWTH ABILITIES IN NATURE.

PLANTS IN THE GREENHOUSE ARE NOW WIRED UP LIKE *SUPERCOMPUTERS.* FLORA THAT WOULD TAKE YEARS TO GROW AND MATURE NOW EVOLVE IN DAYS.

SILAS IS NOW IN DANGER! I CAN'T ALERT THE AUTHORITIES-- HIS LIFE'S WORK COULD FALL INTO THE WRONG HANDS. YOU'RE HIS ONLY HOPE OF MAKING IT OUT OF THERE *ALIVE!*

OF *COURSE* WE'LL LOOK FOR UNCLE SILAS!

YOU BET!

WE MUST WORK QUICKLY-- GET A POD SUIT EACH.

SUITS? FROM WHERE?

I THINK SHE MEANS *THESE* THINGS...

PLUCK

EEEEEEKKK!!

SELENA

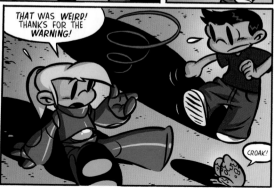

THAT WAS *WEIRD!* THANKS FOR THE *WARNING!*

CROAK!

9

THIS IS COOL! I CAN'T WAIT TO SEE WHAT IT CAN DO!

YOUR TURN, TOMMY!

ARE YOU *CRAZY?!*

CROAK!

THE POD SUITS AREN'T HARMFUL; THEY WILL *PROTECT* YOU. THEY ARE ALSO THE ONLY WAY TO *CONTACT* YOU ONCE YOU'RE INSIDE THE FOREST.

WELL, *SORRY* FOR TAKING MY TIME!

PLUCK

YOUNGER BROTHERS CAN BE THE BIGGEST *WHINGERS.*

FMP!

CLICK

I'LL GET YOU BACK FOR THAT. JUST YOU WAIT...

WHATEVER YOU *RECKON.*

WUMF

YOU MUST HURRY! I'LL CONTACT YOU ONCE YOU'RE THROUGH THE DOOR.

WE CAN STILL TELL MUM AND DAD ABOUT THIS, YOU KNOW.

BONK!

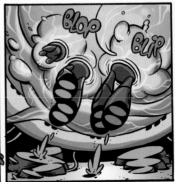

NAAAHH!

LAST ONE THROUGH IS A ROTTEN EGG!

YOU SMELL ENOUGH *NOW!*

BLOP

BLIP

CROAK!

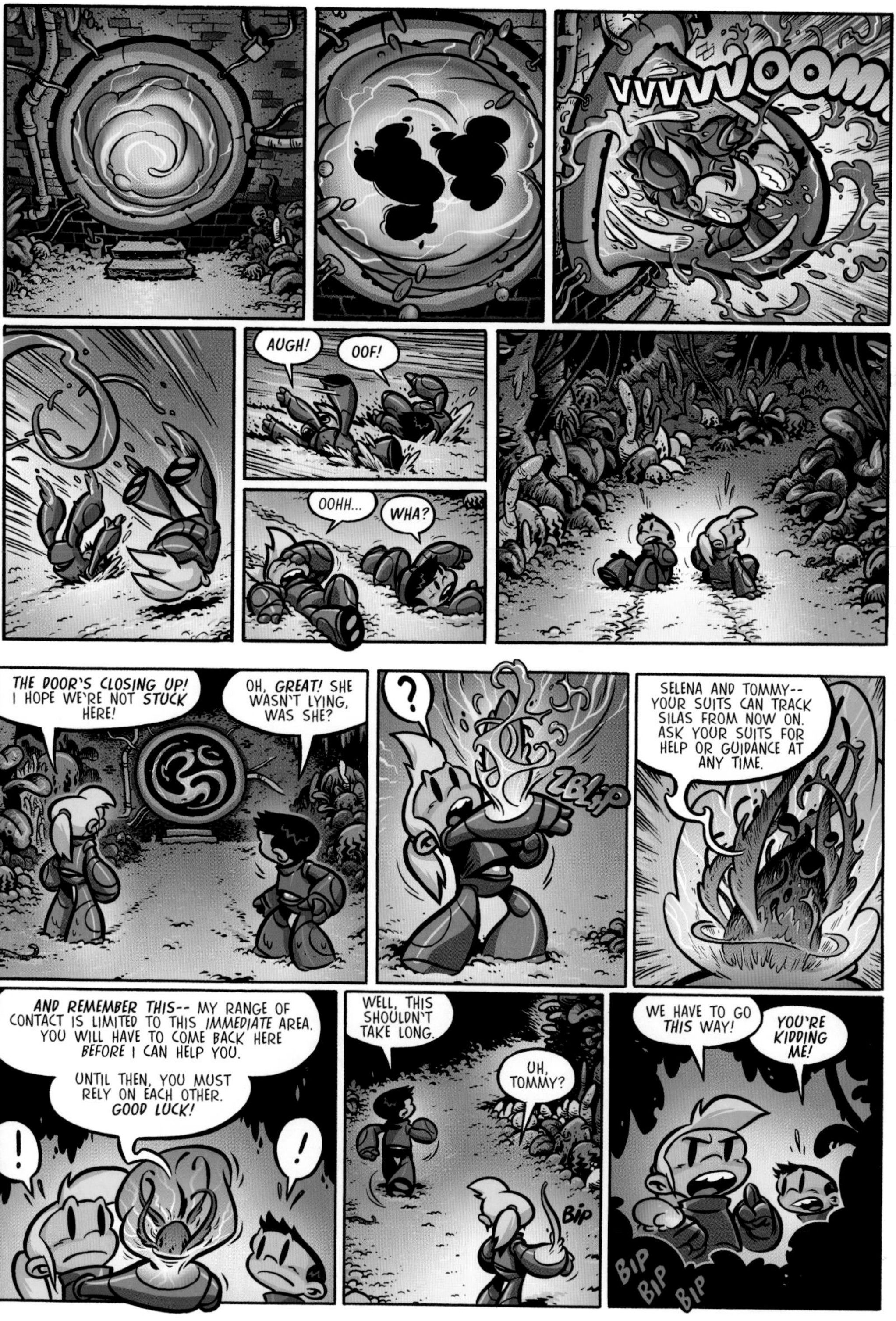
VVVVVOOM!
AUGH!
OOF!
OOHH...
WHA?
THE DOOR'S CLOSING UP! I HOPE WE'RE NOT STUCK HERE!
OH, GREAT! SHE WASN'T LYING, WAS SHE?
?
ZBLIP
SELENA AND TOMMY-- YOUR SUITS CAN TRACK SILAS FROM NOW ON. ASK YOUR SUITS FOR HELP OR GUIDANCE AT ANY TIME.
AND REMEMBER THIS-- MY RANGE OF CONTACT IS LIMITED TO THIS IMMEDIATE AREA. YOU WILL HAVE TO COME BACK HERE BEFORE I CAN HELP YOU.
UNTIL THEN, YOU MUST RELY ON EACH OTHER. GOOD LUCK!
!
!
WELL, THIS SHOULDN'T TAKE LONG.
UH, TOMMY?
BIP
WE HAVE TO GO THIS WAY!
YOU'RE KIDDING ME!
BIP
BIP
BIP

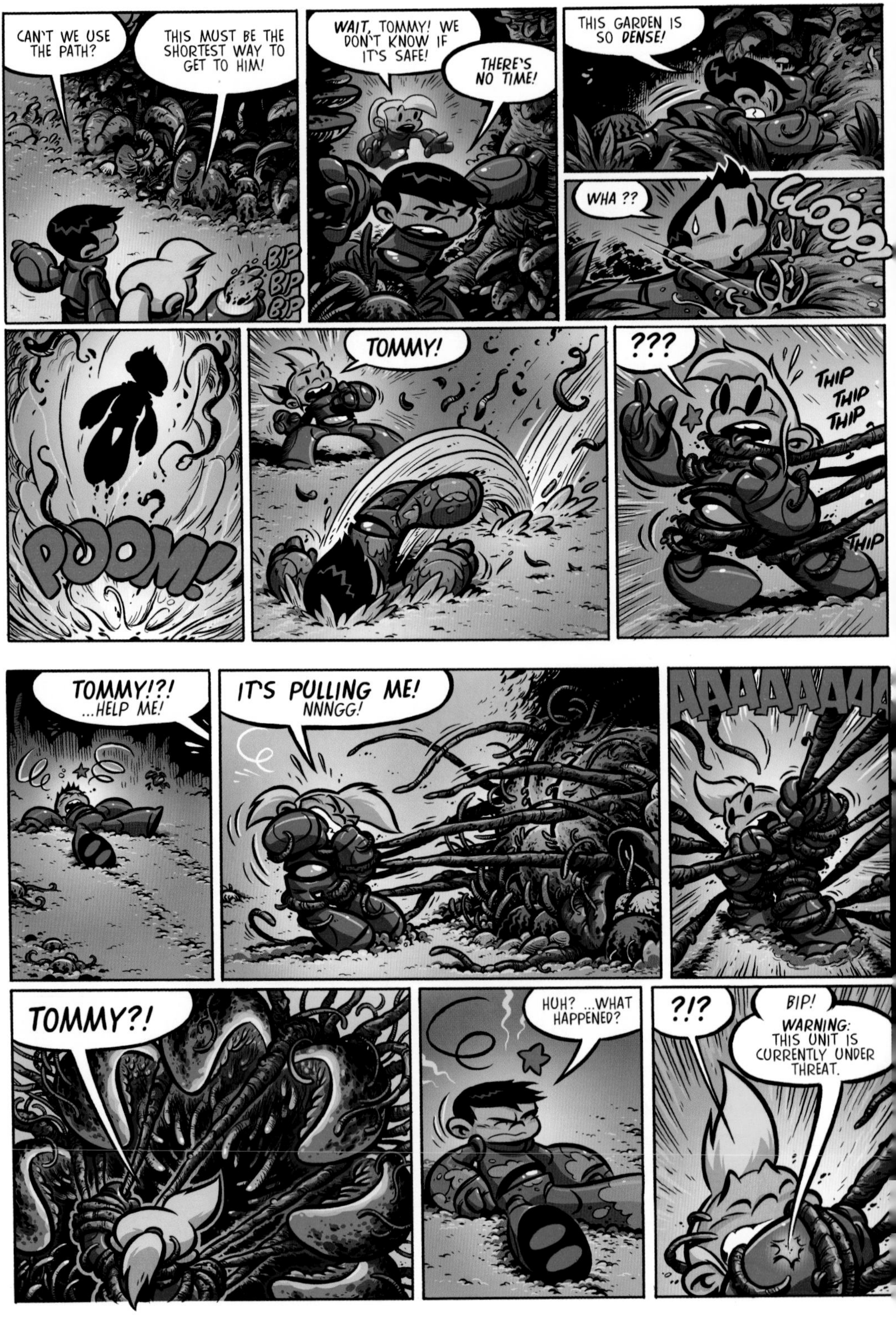
CAN'T WE USE THE PATH?
THIS MUST BE THE SHORTEST WAY TO GET TO HIM!
BIP BIP BIP
WAIT, TOMMY! WE DON'T KNOW IF IT'S SAFE!
THERE'S NO TIME!
THIS GARDEN IS SO DENSE!
WHA ??
GLOOP!
POOM!
TOMMY!
???
THIP THIP THIP
THIP
TOMMY!?!
...HELP ME!
IT'S PULLING ME!
NNNGG!
AAAAAAA
TOMMY?!
HUH? ...WHAT HAPPENED?
?!?
BIP!
WARNING: THIS UNIT IS CURRENTLY UNDER THREAT.

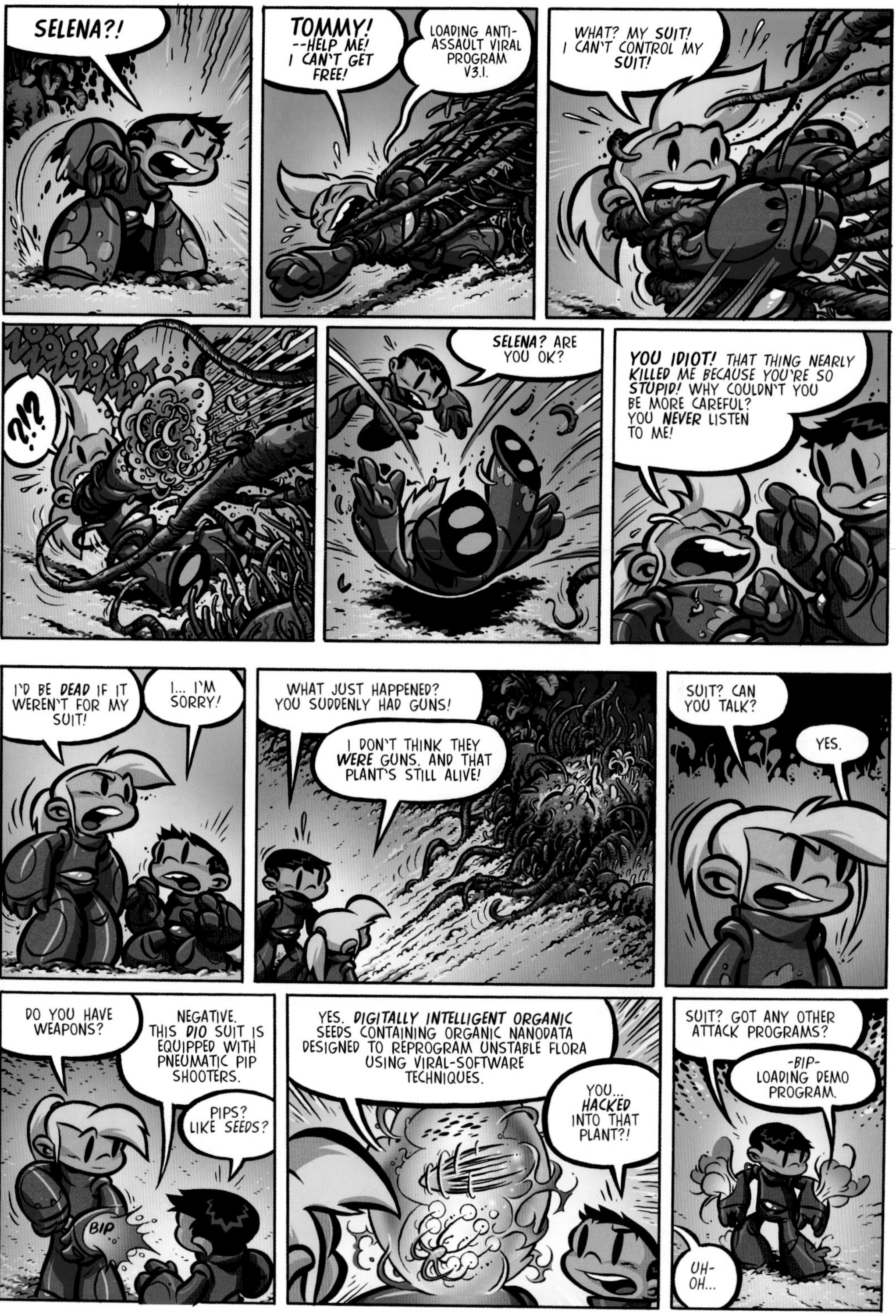
SELENA?!
TOMMY! --HELP ME! I CAN'T GET FREE!
LOADING ANTI-ASSAULT VIRAL PROGRAM V3.1.
WHAT? MY SUIT! I CAN'T CONTROL MY SUIT!
ZOT ZOT ZOT
?!?
SELENA? ARE YOU OK?
YOU IDIOT! THAT THING NEARLY KILLED ME BECAUSE YOU'RE SO STUPID! WHY COULDN'T YOU BE MORE CAREFUL? YOU NEVER LISTEN TO ME!
I'D BE DEAD IF IT WEREN'T FOR MY SUIT!
I... I'M SORRY!
WHAT JUST HAPPENED? YOU SUDDENLY HAD GUNS!
I DON'T THINK THEY WERE GUNS. AND THAT PLANT'S STILL ALIVE!
SUIT? CAN YOU TALK?
YES.
DO YOU HAVE WEAPONS?
NEGATIVE. THIS DIO SUIT IS EQUIPPED WITH PNEUMATIC PIP SHOOTERS.
PIPS? LIKE SEEDS?
BIP
YES. DIGITALLY INTELLIGENT ORGANIC SEEDS CONTAINING ORGANIC NANODATA DESIGNED TO REPROGRAM UNSTABLE FLORA USING VIRAL-SOFTWARE TECHNIQUES.
YOU... HACKED INTO THAT PLANT?!
SUIT? GOT ANY OTHER ATTACK PROGRAMS?
-BIP- LOADING DEMO PROGRAM.
UH-OH...

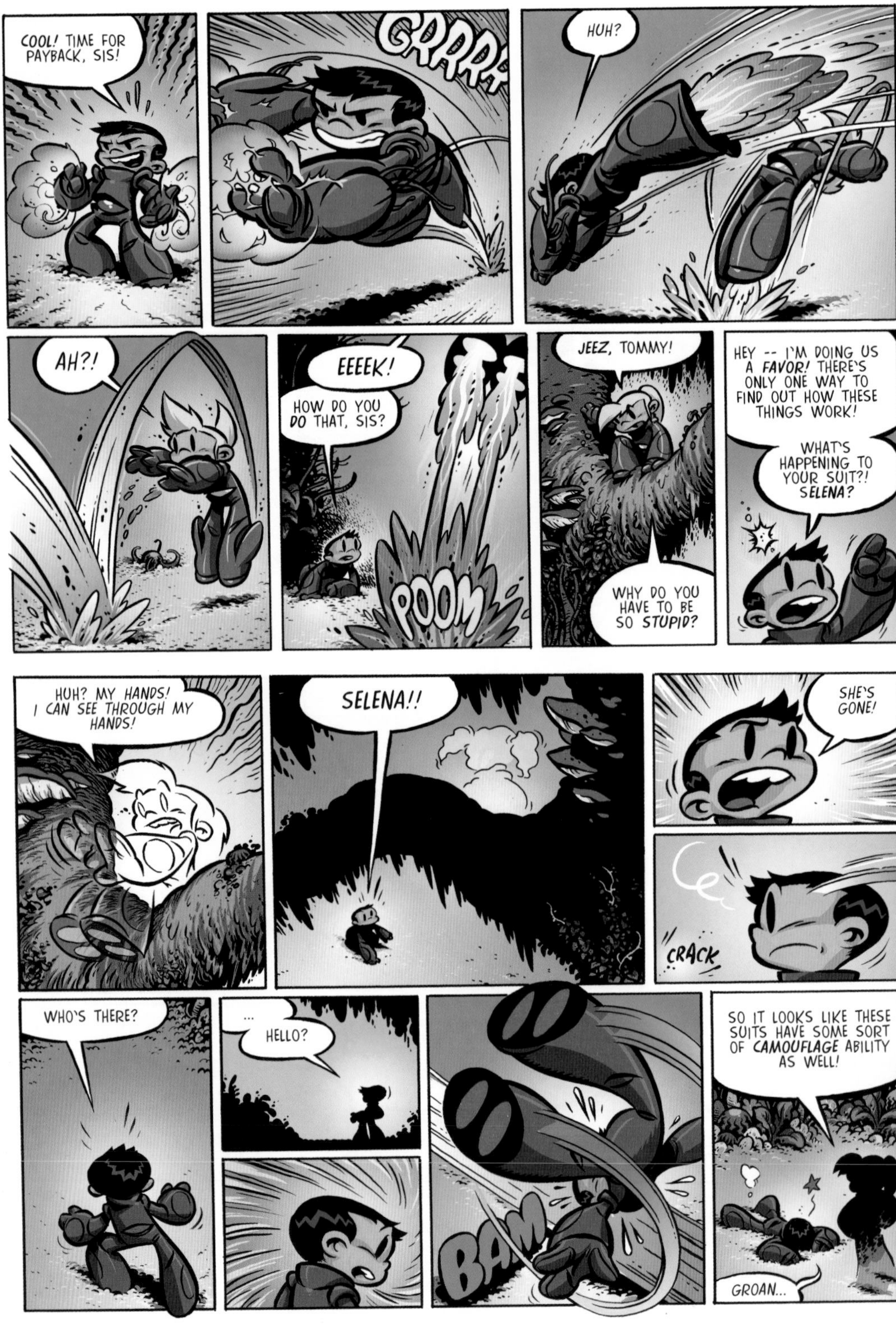
COOL! TIME FOR PAYBACK, SIS!
GRRRR
HUH?
AH?!
EEEEK!
HOW DO YOU DO THAT, SIS?
POOM
JEEZ, TOMMY!
WHY DO YOU HAVE TO BE SO STUPID?
HEY -- I'M DOING US A FAVOR! THERE'S ONLY ONE WAY TO FIND OUT HOW THESE THINGS WORK!
WHAT'S HAPPENING TO YOUR SUIT?! SELENA?
HUH? MY HANDS! I CAN SEE THROUGH MY HANDS!
SELENA!!
SHE'S GONE!
CRACK
WHO'S THERE?
... HELLO?
BAM
SO IT LOOKS LIKE THESE SUITS HAVE SOME SORT OF CAMOUFLAGE ABILITY AS WELL!
GROAN...

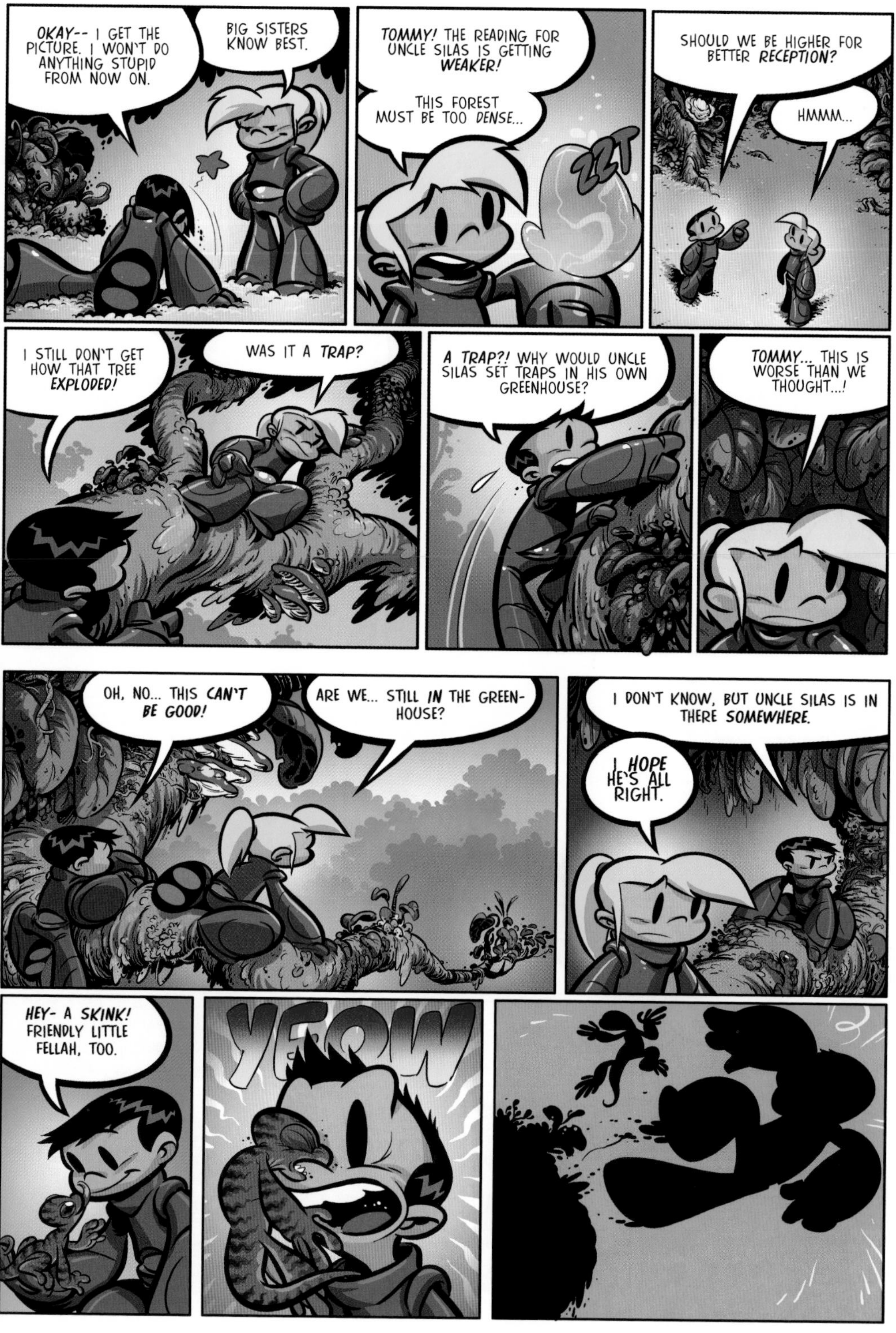
OKAY-- I GET THE PICTURE. I WON'T DO ANYTHING STUPID FROM NOW ON.
BIG SISTERS KNOW BEST.
TOMMY! THE READING FOR UNCLE SILAS IS GETTING WEAKER!
THIS FOREST MUST BE TOO DENSE...
ZZT
SHOULD WE BE HIGHER FOR BETTER RECEPTION?
HMMM...
I STILL DON'T GET HOW THAT TREE EXPLODED!
WAS IT A TRAP?
A TRAP?! WHY WOULD UNCLE SILAS SET TRAPS IN HIS OWN GREENHOUSE?
TOMMY... THIS IS WORSE THAN WE THOUGHT...!
OH, NO... THIS CAN'T BE GOOD!
ARE WE... STILL IN THE GREEN-HOUSE?
I DON'T KNOW, BUT UNCLE SILAS IS IN THERE SOMEWHERE.
I HOPE HE'S ALL RIGHT.
HEY- A SKINK! FRIENDLY LITTLE FELLAH, TOO.
YEOW

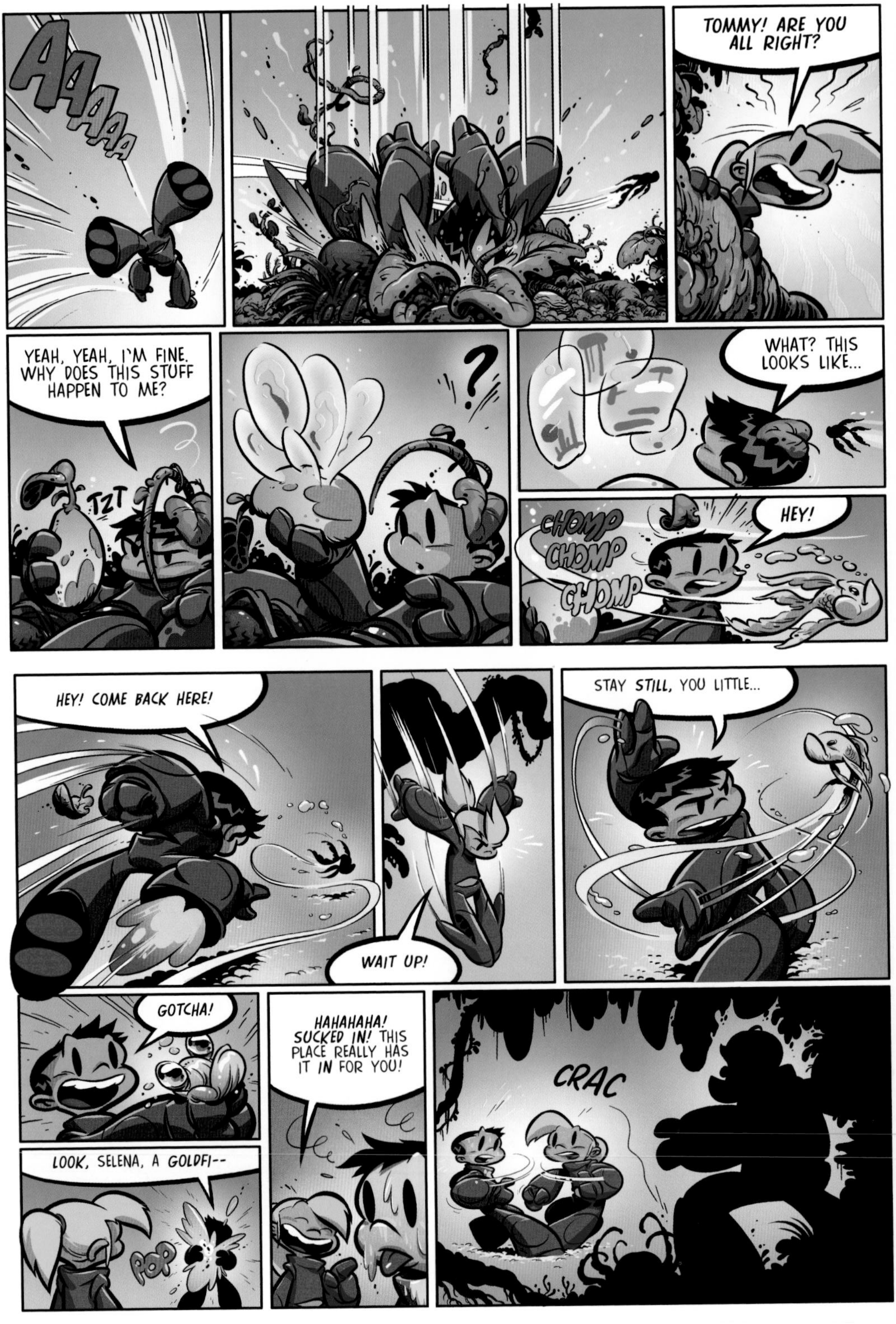
AAAAAA
TOMMY! ARE YOU ALL RIGHT?
YEAH, YEAH, I'M FINE. WHY DOES THIS STUFF HAPPEN TO ME?
TZT
?
WHAT? THIS LOOKS LIKE...
CHOMP CHOMP CHOMP
HEY!
HEY! COME BACK HERE!
WAIT UP!
STAY STILL, YOU LITTLE...
GOTCHA!
LOOK, SELENA, A GOLDFI--
POP
HAHAHAHA! SUCKED IN! THIS PLACE REALLY HAS IT IN FOR YOU!
CRAC

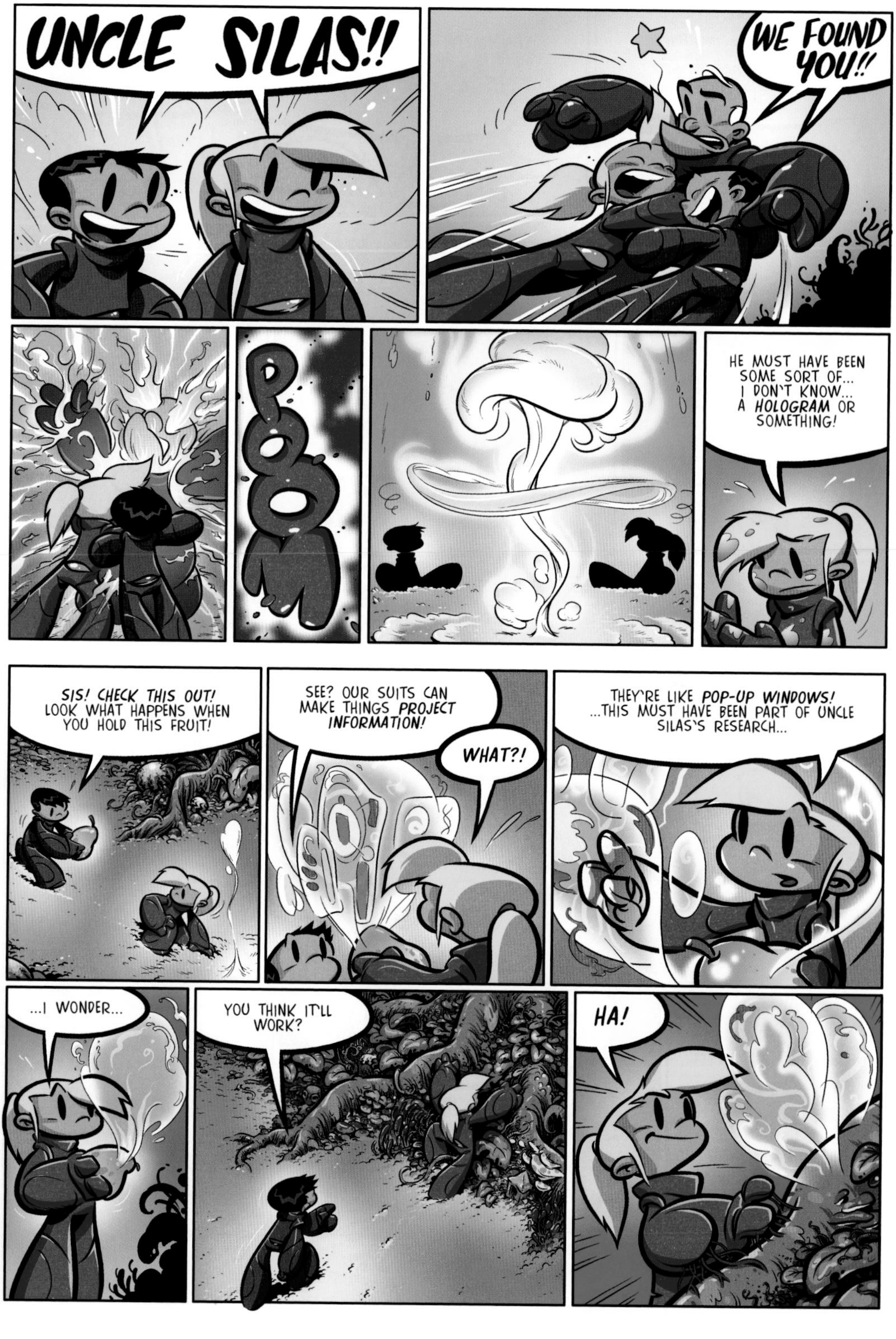
UNCLE SILAS!!
WE FOUND YOU!!
POOM
HE MUST HAVE BEEN SOME SORT OF... I DON'T KNOW... A HOLOGRAM OR SOMETHING!
SIS! CHECK THIS OUT! LOOK WHAT HAPPENS WHEN YOU HOLD THIS FRUIT!
SEE? OUR SUITS CAN MAKE THINGS PROJECT INFORMATION!
WHAT?!
THEY'RE LIKE POP-UP WINDOWS! ...THIS MUST HAVE BEEN PART OF UNCLE SILAS'S RESEARCH...
...I WONDER...
YOU THINK IT'LL WORK?
HA!

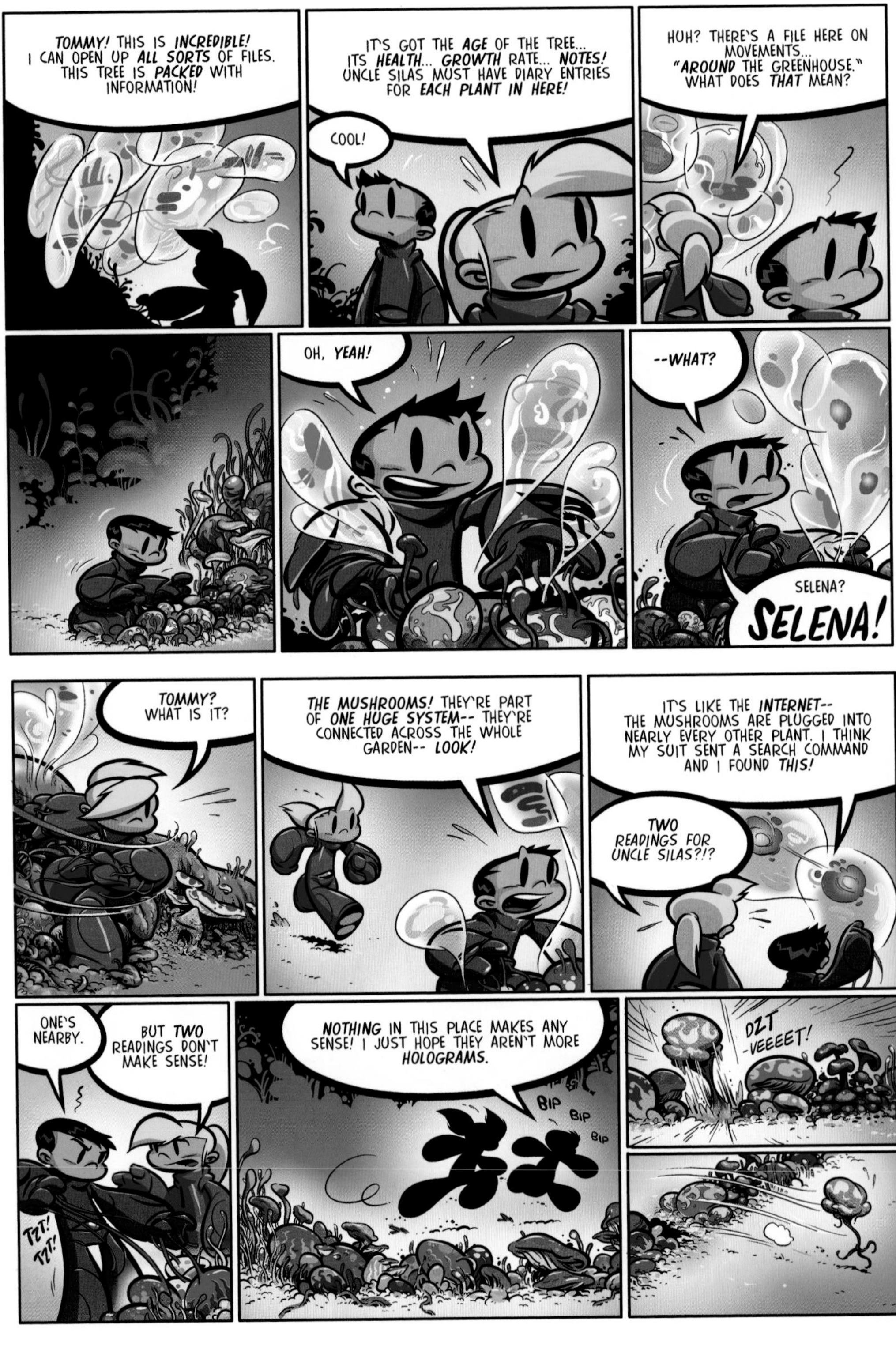
TOMMY! THIS IS INCREDIBLE! I CAN OPEN UP ALL SORTS OF FILES. THIS TREE IS PACKED WITH INFORMATION!
IT'S GOT THE AGE OF THE TREE... ITS HEALTH... GROWTH RATE... NOTES! UNCLE SILAS MUST HAVE DIARY ENTRIES FOR EACH PLANT IN HERE!
COOL!
HUH? THERE'S A FILE HERE ON MOVEMENTS... "AROUND THE GREENHOUSE." WHAT DOES THAT MEAN?
OH, YEAH!
--WHAT?
SELENA?
SELENA!
TOMMY? WHAT IS IT?
THE MUSHROOMS! THEY'RE PART OF ONE HUGE SYSTEM-- THEY'RE CONNECTED ACROSS THE WHOLE GARDEN-- LOOK!
IT'S LIKE THE INTERNET-- THE MUSHROOMS ARE PLUGGED INTO NEARLY EVERY OTHER PLANT. I THINK MY SUIT SENT A SEARCH COMMAND AND I FOUND THIS!
TWO READINGS FOR UNCLE SILAS?!?
ONE'S NEARBY.
BUT TWO READINGS DON'T MAKE SENSE!
TZT! TZT!
NOTHING IN THIS PLACE MAKES ANY SENSE! I JUST HOPE THEY AREN'T MORE HOLOGRAMS.
BIP BIP BIP
DZT -VEEEET!

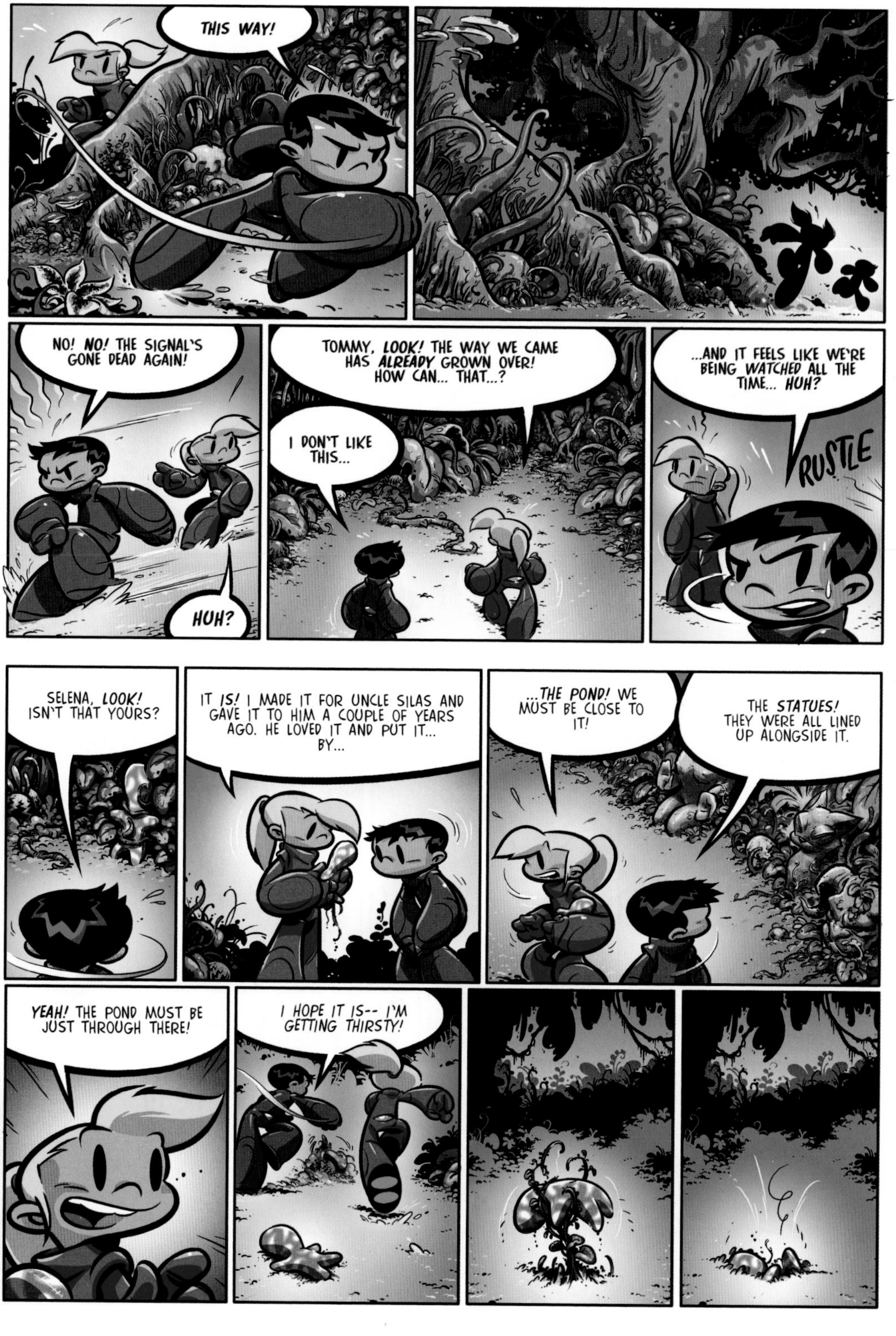

THIS WAY!
NO! NO! THE SIGNAL'S GONE DEAD AGAIN!
HUH?
TOMMY, LOOK! THE WAY WE CAME HAS ALREADY GROWN OVER! HOW CAN... THAT...?
I DON'T LIKE THIS...
...AND IT FEELS LIKE WE'RE BEING WATCHED ALL THE TIME... HUH?
RUSTLE
SELENA, LOOK! ISN'T THAT YOURS?
IT IS! I MADE IT FOR UNCLE SILAS AND GAVE IT TO HIM A COUPLE OF YEARS AGO. HE LOVED IT AND PUT IT... BY...
...THE POND! WE MUST BE CLOSE TO IT!
THE STATUES! THEY WERE ALL LINED UP ALONGSIDE IT.
YEAH! THE POND MUST BE JUST THROUGH THERE!
I HOPE IT IS-- I'M GETTING THIRSTY!

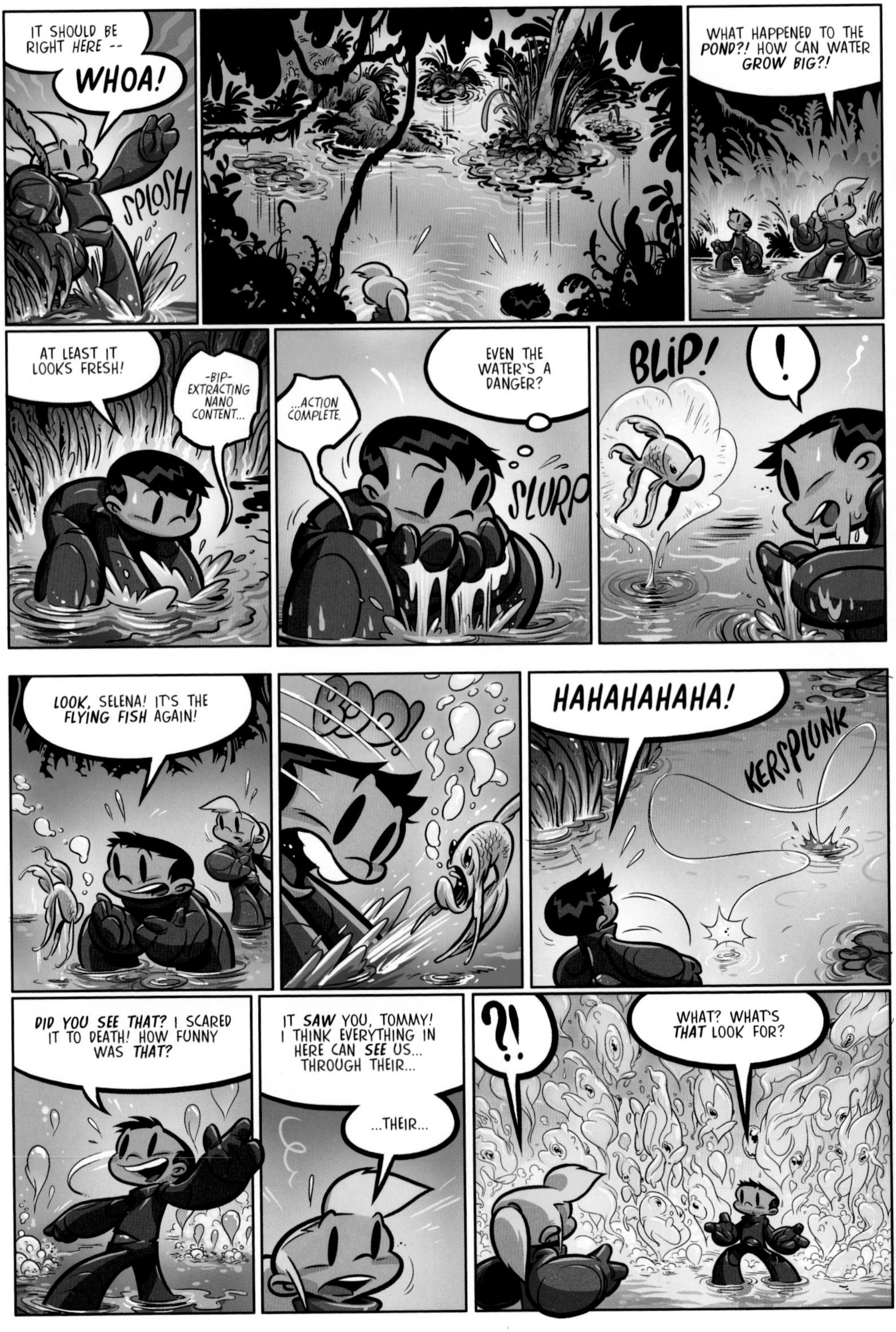
IT SHOULD BE RIGHT HERE --
WHOA!
SPLOSH
WHAT HAPPENED TO THE POND?! HOW CAN WATER GROW BIG?!
AT LEAST IT LOOKS FRESH!
-BIP- EXTRACTING NANO CONTENT...
...ACTION COMPLETE.
EVEN THE WATER'S A DANGER?
SLURP
BLIP!
!
LOOK, SELENA! IT'S THE FLYING FISH AGAIN!
HAHAHAHAHA!
KERSPLUNK
DID YOU SEE THAT? I SCARED IT TO DEATH! HOW FUNNY WAS THAT?
IT SAW YOU, TOMMY! I THINK EVERYTHING IN HERE CAN SEE US... THROUGH THEIR...
...THEIR...
?!
WHAT? WHAT'S THAT LOOK FOR?

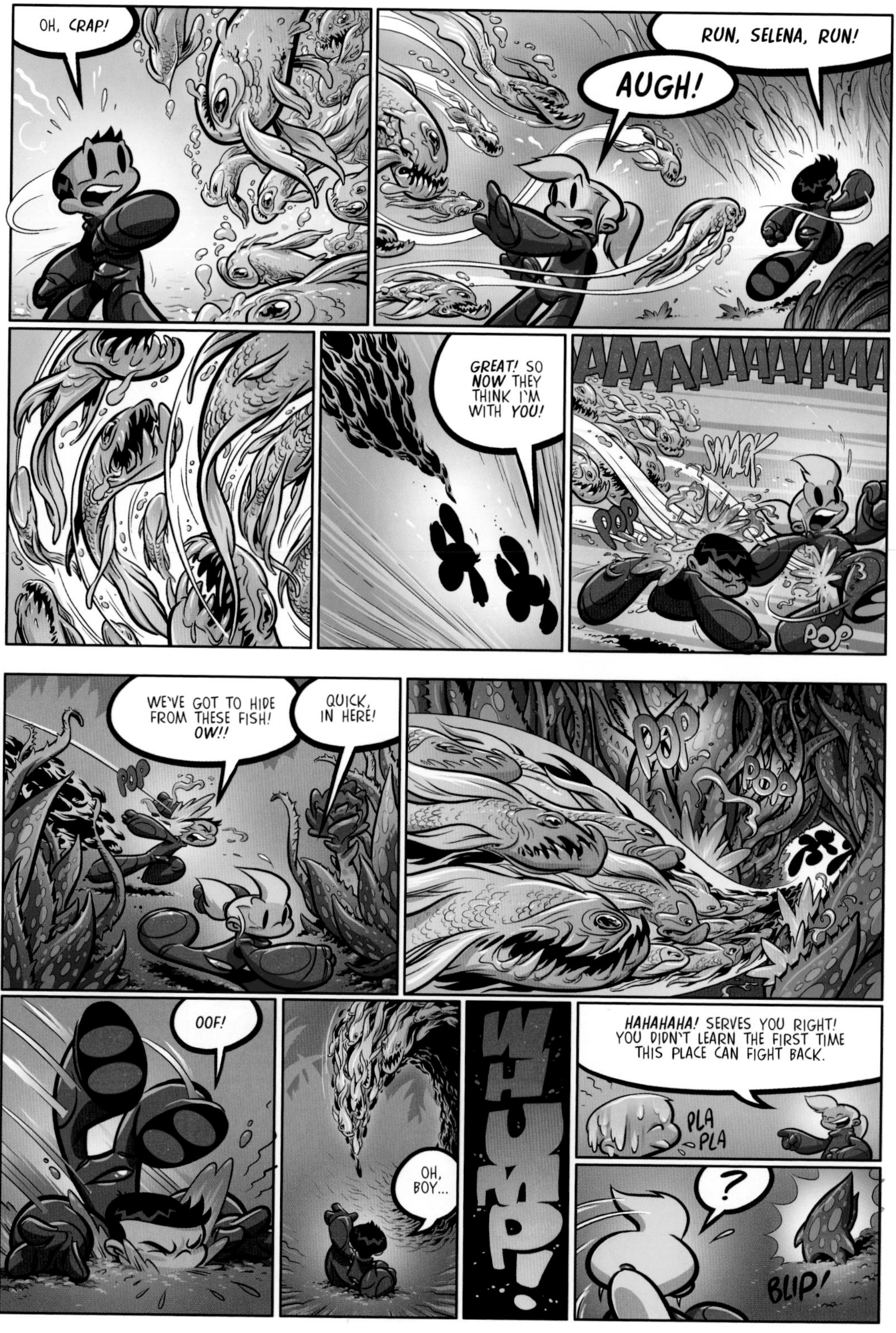
OH, CRAP!
RUN, SELENA, RUN!
AUGH!
GREAT! SO NOW THEY THINK I'M WITH YOU!
AAAAAAAAAAAA
SMACK
POP
POP
WE'VE GOT TO HIDE FROM THESE FISH! OW!!
QUICK, IN HERE!
POP
POP
POP
OOF!
OH, BOY...
WHUMP!
HAHAHAHA! SERVES YOU RIGHT! YOU DIDN'T LEARN THE FIRST TIME THIS PLACE CAN FIGHT BACK.
PLA PLA
?
BLIP!

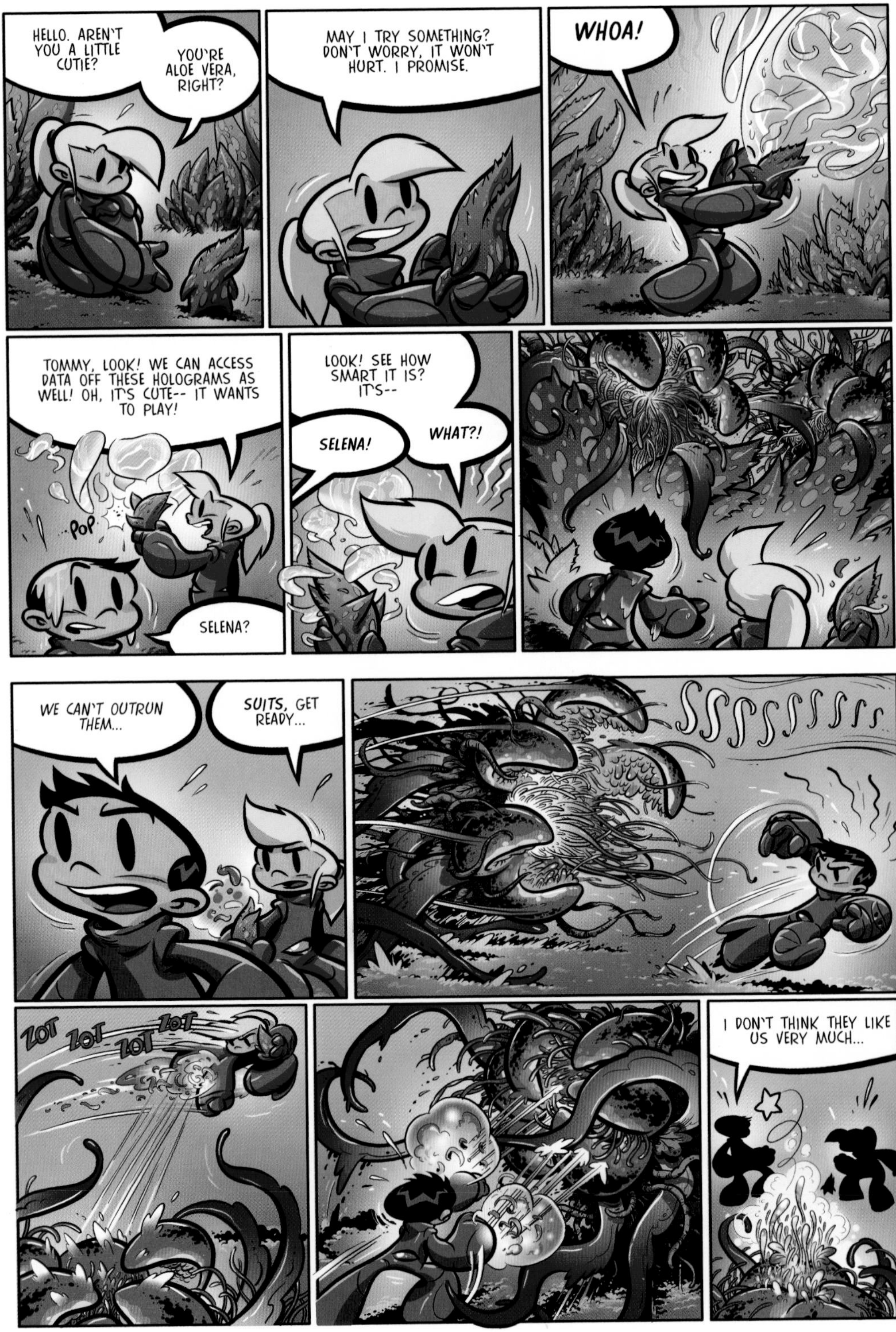
HELLO. AREN'T YOU A LITTLE CUTIE?
YOU'RE ALOE VERA, RIGHT?
MAY I TRY SOMETHING? DON'T WORRY, IT WON'T HURT. I PROMISE.
WHOA!
TOMMY, LOOK! WE CAN ACCESS DATA OFF THESE HOLOGRAMS AS WELL! OH, IT'S CUTE-- IT WANTS TO PLAY!
...POP
SELENA?
LOOK! SEE HOW SMART IT IS? IT'S--
SELENA!
WHAT?!
WE CAN'T OUTRUN THEM...
SUITS, GET READY...
SSSSSSSSS
ZOT ZOT ZOT ZOT
I DON'T THINK THEY LIKE US VERY MUCH...

SOFIA? JUST HOW BIG *IS* THIS GARDEN?

-BIP- UNKNOWN. MORE DATA NEEDED.

"MORE DATA"? ...*MUSHROOMS!* I NEED TO FIND... *THERE!*

MUSHROOMS SEEM TO KNOW EVERYTHING.

IS THERE ANY SORT OF *CENTER* TO THE FOREST?

I THINK SO!

TOMMY, THAT'S A *FIBONACCI* SPIRAL! I LEARNED ABOUT IT IN MATH.

A FIBBER-*WHAT?*

IT'S A MAP OF THE MUSHROOMS. *SEE?* THEY MUST SPIRAL INTO THE MIDDLE OF THE GARDEN.

IT'S GETTING PRETTY DARK. WE SHOULD FIND A PLACE TO *SLEEP* TONIGHT. WE'LL FOLLOW THE SPIRAL IN THE MORNING.

I HOPE UNCLE SILAS IS ALL RIGHT...

I'VE NEVER EATEN FRUIT THAT *GLOWS* BEFORE.

TASTES GOOD, TOO! BUUURP

WE'LL HAVE TO TAKE TURNS TO *KEEP WATCH* TONIGHT, TOMMY. THERE ARE *ALL SORTS* OF *WEIRD PLANTS* OUT THERE.

WAKE ME UP IN... THREE HOURS... OK?

DON'T WORRY, SIS. YOU CAN COUNT ON ME...

TO WATCH...

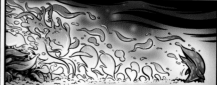

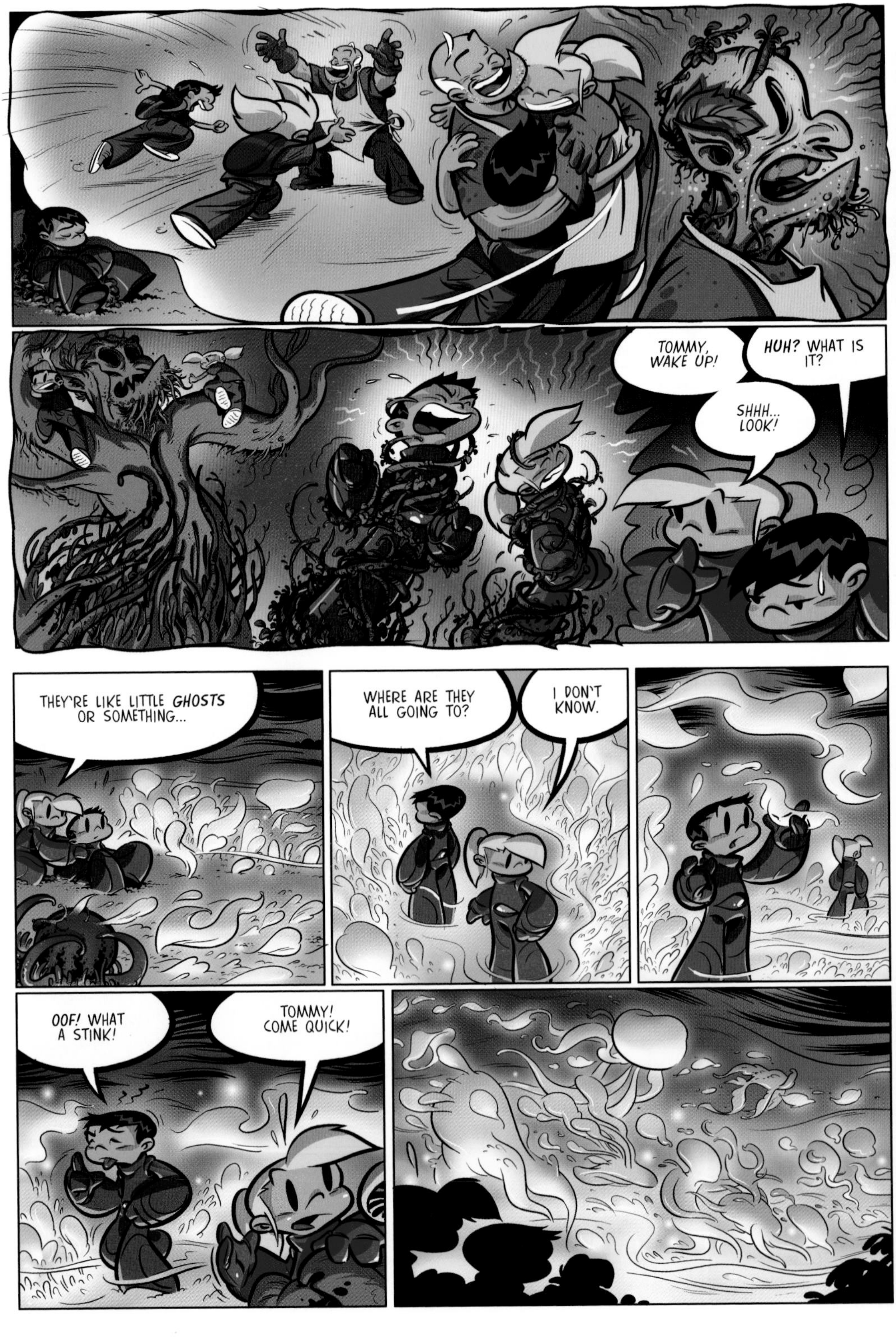
TOMMY, WAKE UP!
HUH? WHAT IS IT?
SHHH... LOOK!
THEY'RE LIKE LITTLE GHOSTS OR SOMETHING...
WHERE ARE THEY ALL GOING TO?
I DON'T KNOW.
OOF! WHAT A STINK!
TOMMY! COME QUICK!

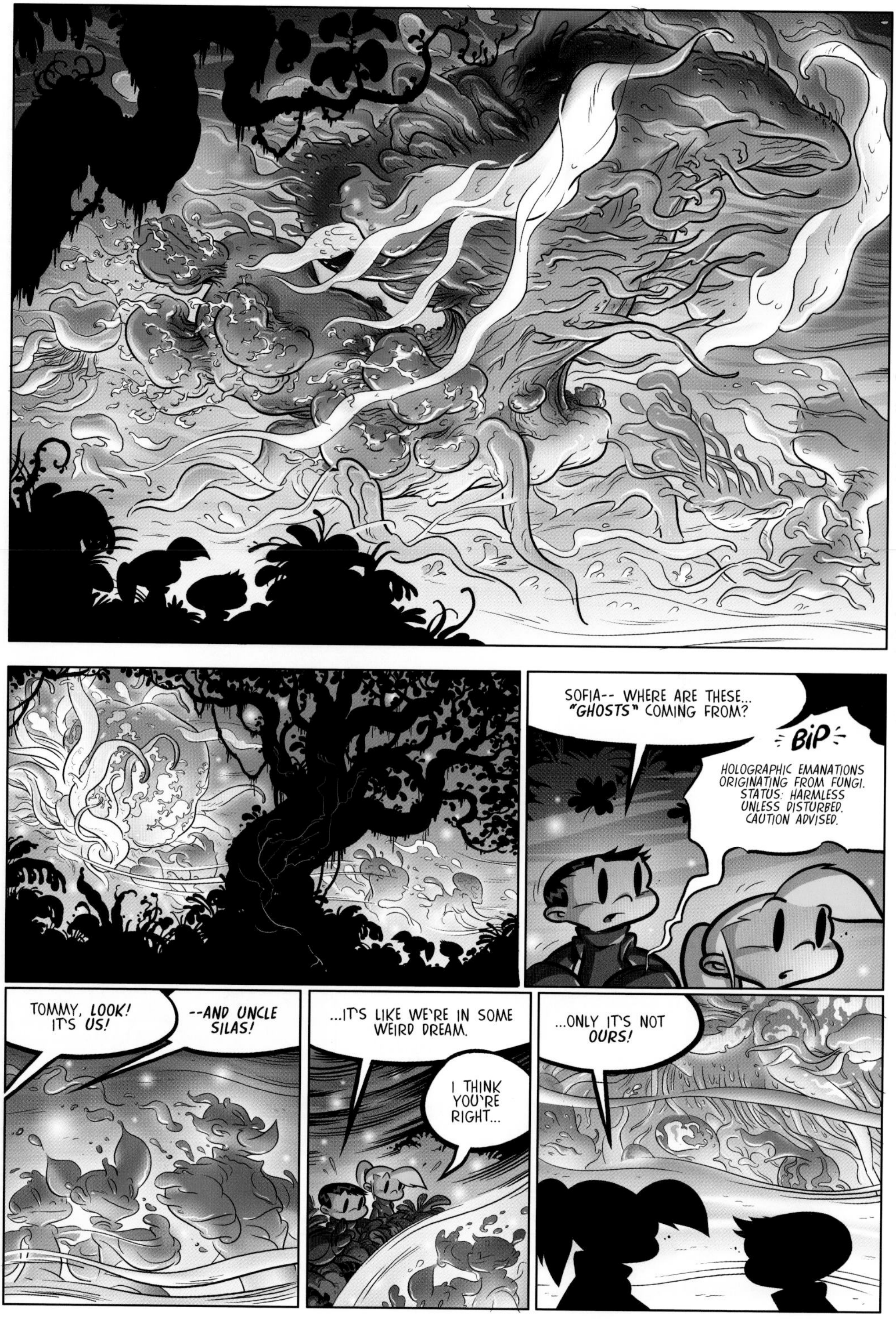
SOFIA-- WHERE ARE THESE... "GHOSTS" COMING FROM?
BIP
HOLOGRAPHIC EMANATIONS ORIGINATING FROM FUNGI. STATUS: HARMLESS UNLESS DISTURBED. CAUTION ADVISED.
TOMMY, LOOK! IT'S US!
--AND UNCLE SILAS!
...IT'S LIKE WE'RE IN SOME WEIRD DREAM.
I THINK YOU'RE RIGHT...
...ONLY IT'S NOT OURS!

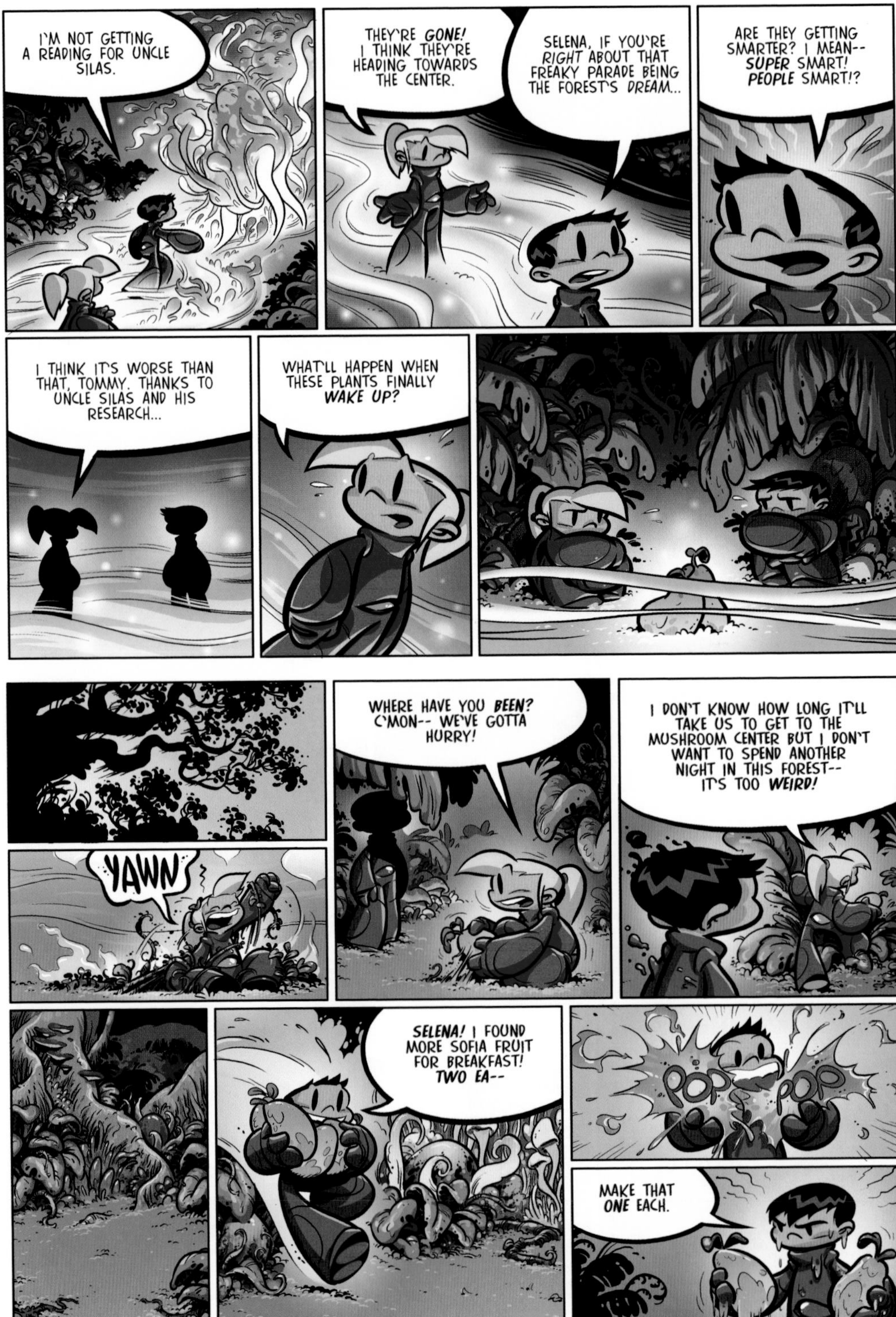
I'M NOT GETTING A READING FOR UNCLE SILAS.
THEY'RE GONE! I THINK THEY'RE HEADING TOWARDS THE CENTER.
SELENA, IF YOU'RE RIGHT ABOUT THAT FREAKY PARADE BEING THE FOREST'S DREAM...
ARE THEY GETTING SMARTER? I MEAN-- SUPER SMART! PEOPLE SMART!?
I THINK IT'S WORSE THAN THAT, TOMMY. THANKS TO UNCLE SILAS AND HIS RESEARCH...
WHAT'LL HAPPEN WHEN THESE PLANTS FINALLY WAKE UP?
YAWN
WHERE HAVE YOU BEEN? C'MON-- WE'VE GOTTA HURRY!
I DON'T KNOW HOW LONG IT'LL TAKE US TO GET TO THE MUSHROOM CENTER BUT I DON'T WANT TO SPEND ANOTHER NIGHT IN THIS FOREST-- IT'S TOO WEIRD!
SELENA! I FOUND MORE SOFIA FRUIT FOR BREAKFAST! TWO EA--
POP
POP
MAKE THAT ONE EACH.

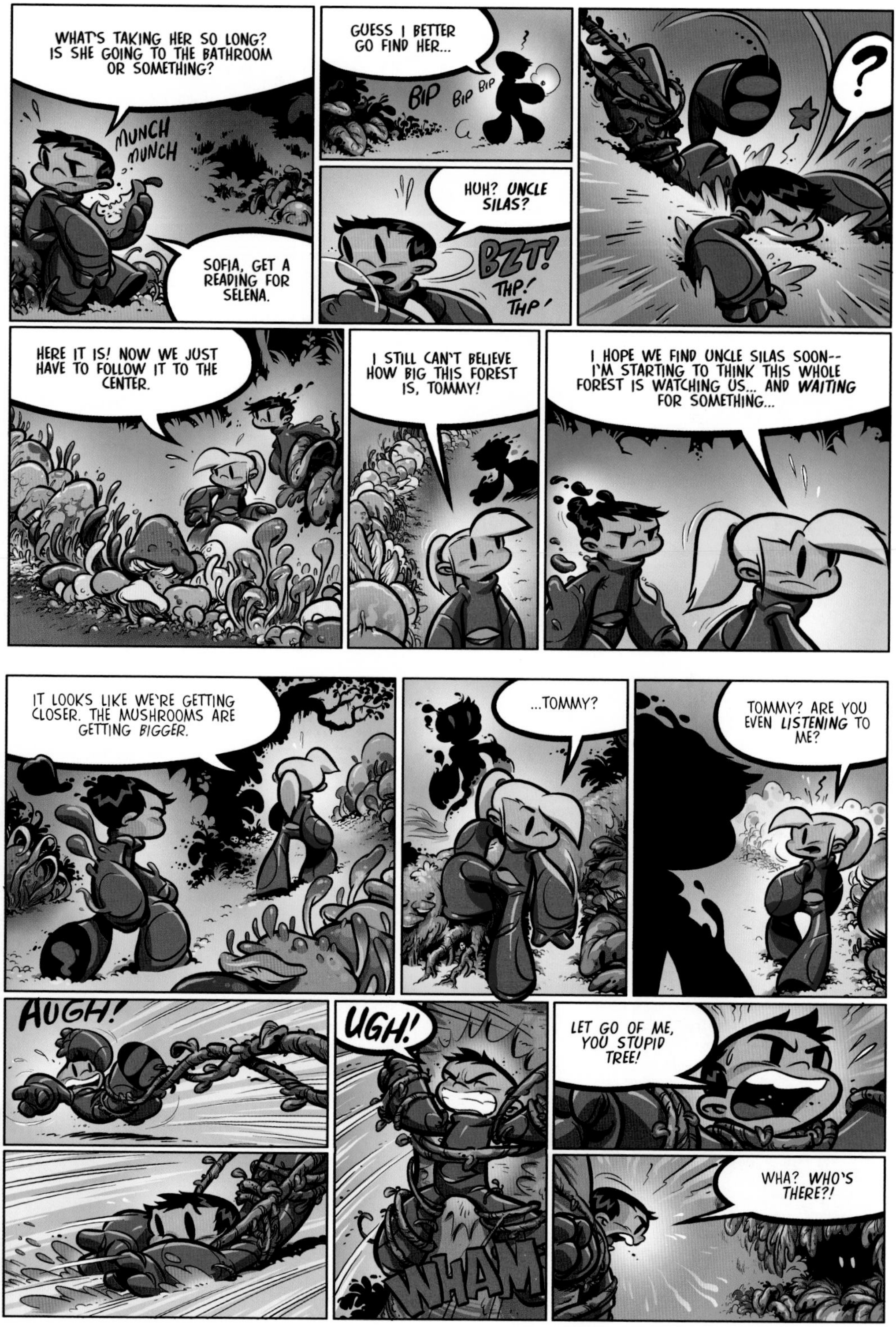
WHAT'S TAKING HER SO LONG? IS SHE GOING TO THE BATHROOM OR SOMETHING?
MUNCH MUNCH
SOFIA, GET A READING FOR SELENA.
GUESS I BETTER GO FIND HER...
BIP BIP BIP
HUH? UNCLE SILAS?
BZT! THP! THP!
?
HERE IT IS! NOW WE JUST HAVE TO FOLLOW IT TO THE CENTER.
I STILL CAN'T BELIEVE HOW BIG THIS FOREST IS, TOMMY!
I HOPE WE FIND UNCLE SILAS SOON-- I'M STARTING TO THINK THIS WHOLE FOREST IS WATCHING US... AND WAITING FOR SOMETHING...
IT LOOKS LIKE WE'RE GETTING CLOSER. THE MUSHROOMS ARE GETTING BIGGER.
...TOMMY?
TOMMY? ARE YOU EVEN LISTENING TO ME?
AUGH!
UGH!
LET GO OF ME, YOU STUPID TREE!
WHAM
WHA? WHO'S THERE?!

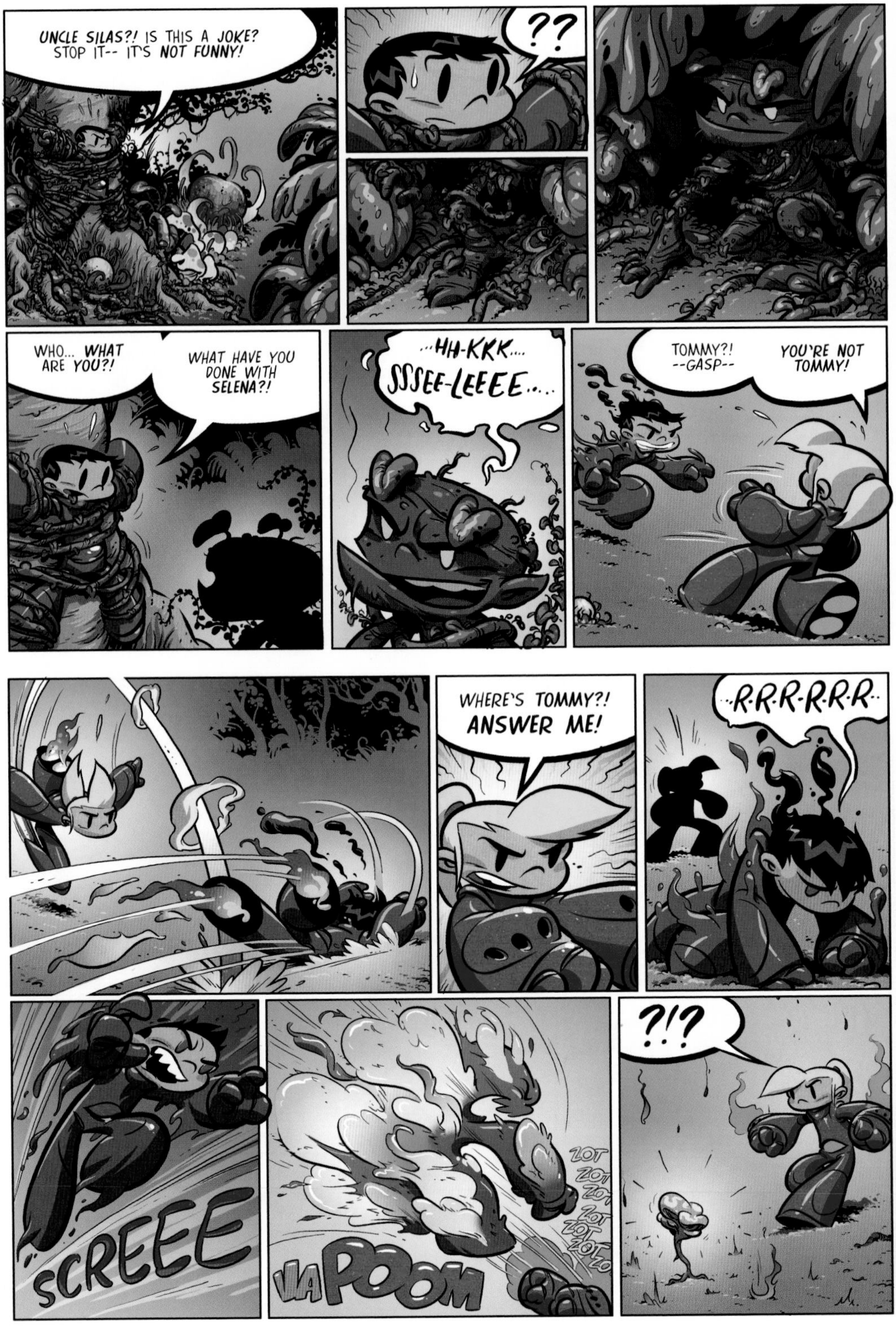
UNCLE SILAS?! IS THIS A JOKE? STOP IT-- IT'S NOT FUNNY!
??
WHO... WHAT ARE YOU?!
WHAT HAVE YOU DONE WITH SELENA?!
...HH-KKK....
SSSEE-LEEEE....
TOMMY?! --GASP--
YOU'RE NOT TOMMY!
WHERE'S TOMMY?! ANSWER ME!
..R-R-R-R-R-R..
SCREEE
VAPOOM
ZOT ZOT ZOT ZOT ZOT ZOT
?!?

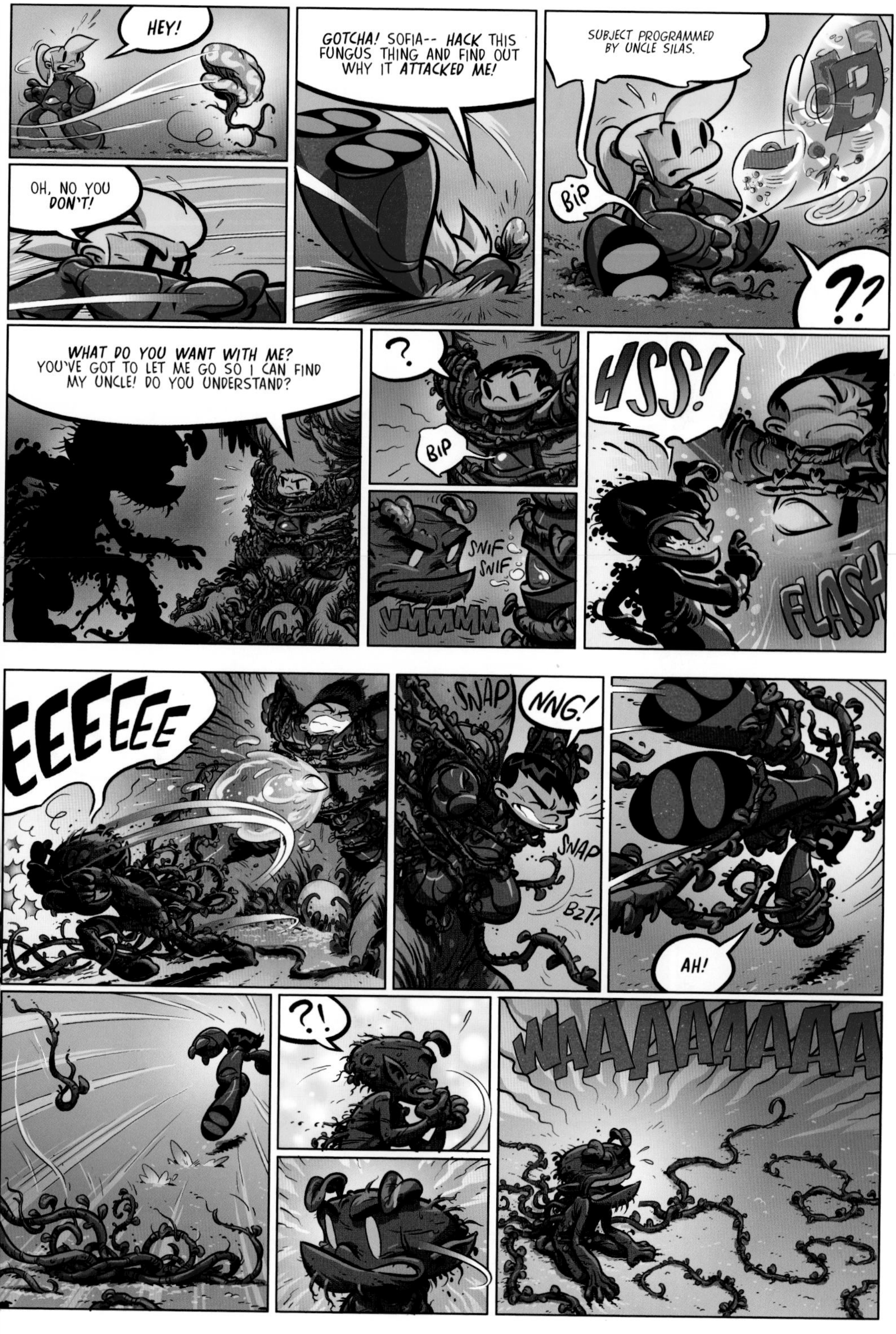
HEY!
OH, NO YOU DON'T!
GOTCHA! SOFIA-- HACK THIS FUNGUS THING AND FIND OUT WHY IT ATTACKED ME!
SUBJECT PROGRAMMED BY UNCLE SILAS.
BIP
??
WHAT DO YOU WANT WITH ME? YOU'VE GOT TO LET ME GO SO I CAN FIND MY UNCLE! DO YOU UNDERSTAND?
?
BIP
SNIF SNIF
VMMMMM
HSS!
FLASH
EEEEEE
SNAP
NNG!
SNAP
BZT!
AH!
?!
WAAAAAAAA

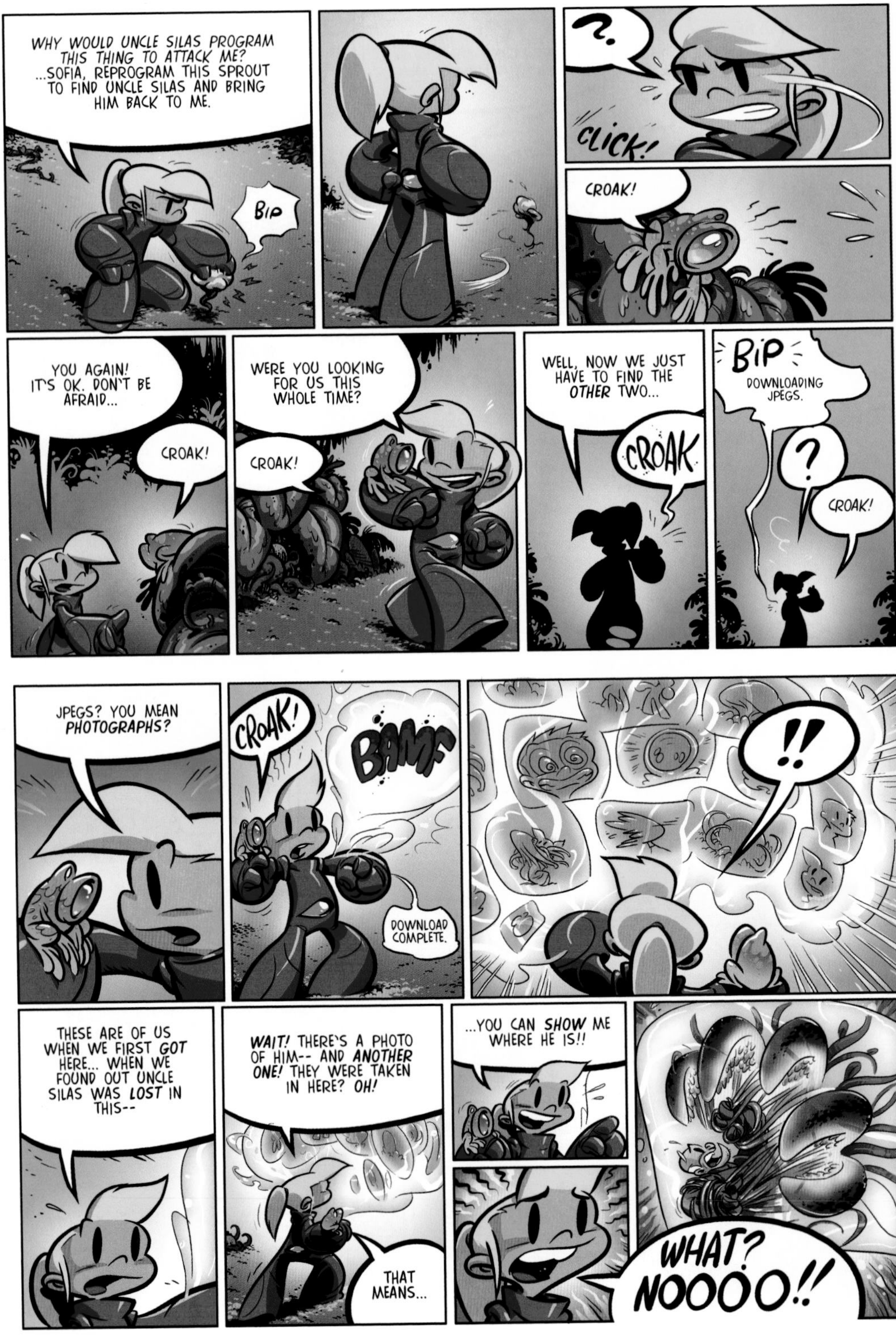
WHY WOULD UNCLE SILAS PROGRAM THIS THING TO ATTACK ME? ...SOFIA, REPROGRAM THIS SPROUT TO FIND UNCLE SILAS AND BRING HIM BACK TO ME.
BIP
?
CLICK!
CROAK!
YOU AGAIN! IT'S OK. DON'T BE AFRAID...
CROAK!
WERE YOU LOOKING FOR US THIS WHOLE TIME?
CROAK!
WELL, NOW WE JUST HAVE TO FIND THE OTHER TWO...
CROAK
BIP
DOWNLOADING JPEGS.
?
CROAK!
JPEGS? YOU MEAN PHOTOGRAPHS?
CROAK!
BAMF
DOWNLOAD COMPLETE.
!!
THESE ARE OF US WHEN WE FIRST GOT HERE... WHEN WE FOUND OUT UNCLE SILAS WAS LOST IN THIS--
WAIT! THERE'S A PHOTO OF HIM-- AND ANOTHER ONE! THEY WERE TAKEN IN HERE? OH!
THAT MEANS...
...YOU CAN SHOW ME WHERE HE IS!!
WHAT? NOOOO!!

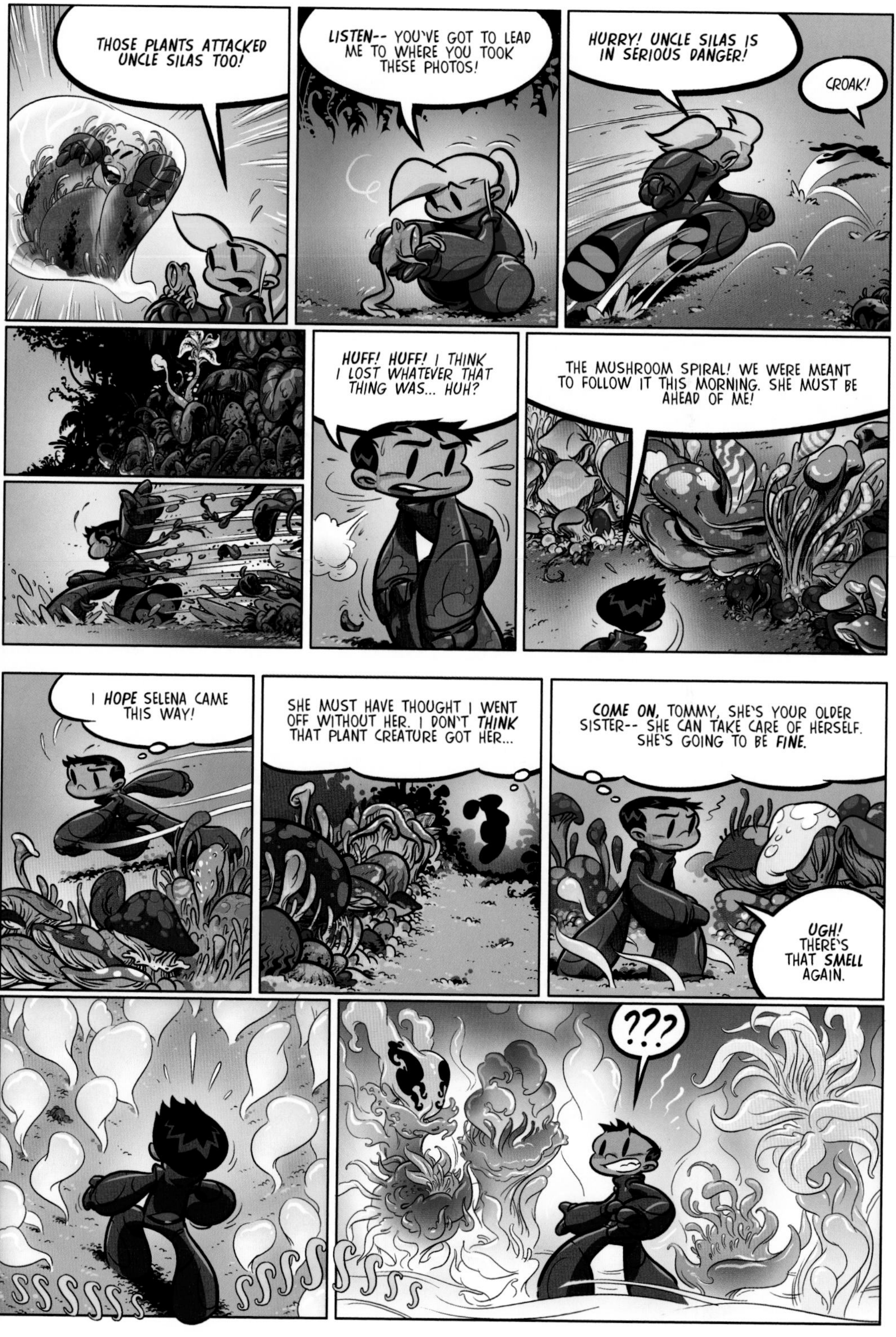
THOSE PLANTS ATTACKED UNCLE SILAS TOO!
LISTEN-- YOU'VE GOT TO LEAD ME TO WHERE YOU TOOK THESE PHOTOS!
HURRY! UNCLE SILAS IS IN SERIOUS DANGER!
CROAK!
HUFF! HUFF! I THINK I LOST WHATEVER THAT THING WAS... HUH?
THE MUSHROOM SPIRAL! WE WERE MEANT TO FOLLOW IT THIS MORNING. SHE MUST BE AHEAD OF ME!
I HOPE SELENA CAME THIS WAY!
SHE MUST HAVE THOUGHT I WENT OFF WITHOUT HER. I DON'T THINK THAT PLANT CREATURE GOT HER...
COME ON, TOMMY, SHE'S YOUR OLDER SISTER-- SHE CAN TAKE CARE OF HERSELF. SHE'S GOING TO BE FINE.
UGH! THERE'S THAT SMELL AGAIN.
???

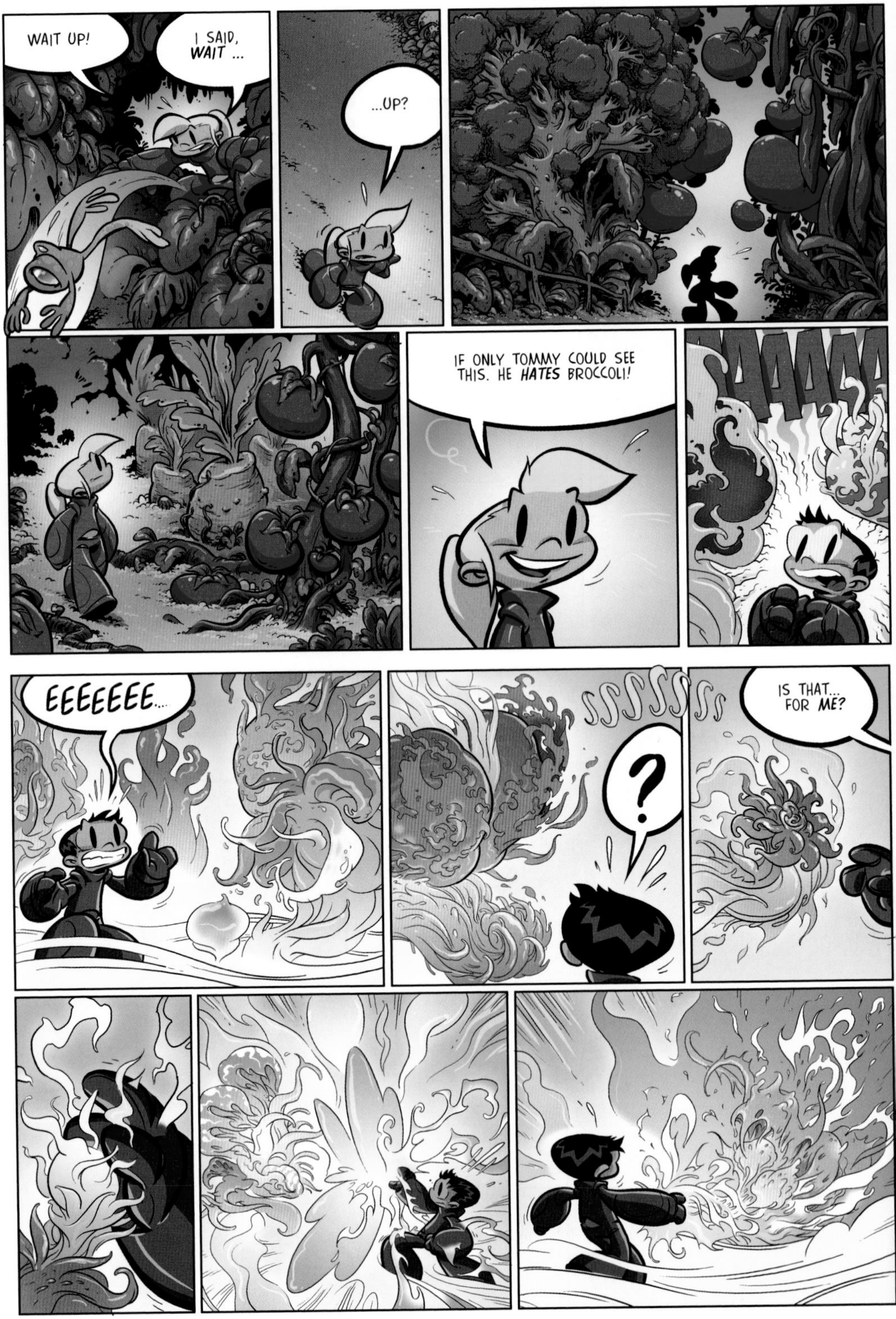
WAIT UP!
I SAID, WAIT ...
...UP?
IF ONLY TOMMY COULD SEE THIS. HE HATES BROCCOLI!
EEEEEEE...
SSSSSSS
?
IS THAT... FOR ME?

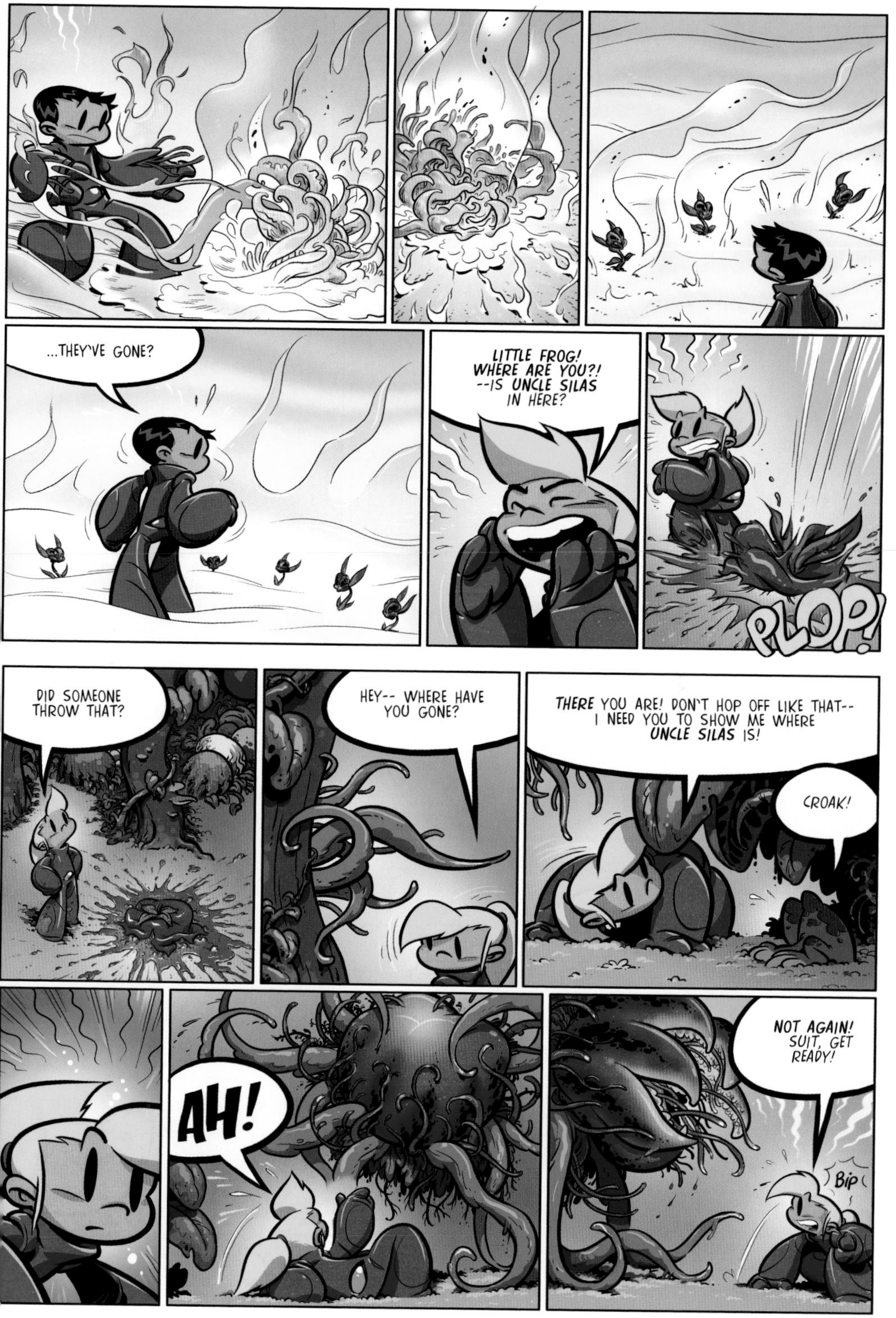
...THEY'VE GONE?
LITTLE FROG! WHERE ARE YOU?! --IS UNCLE SILAS IN HERE?
PLOP!
DID SOMEONE THROW THAT?
HEY-- WHERE HAVE YOU GONE?
THERE YOU ARE! DON'T HOP OFF LIKE THAT-- I NEED YOU TO SHOW ME WHERE UNCLE SILAS IS!
CROAK!
AH!
NOT AGAIN! SUIT, GET READY!
Bip

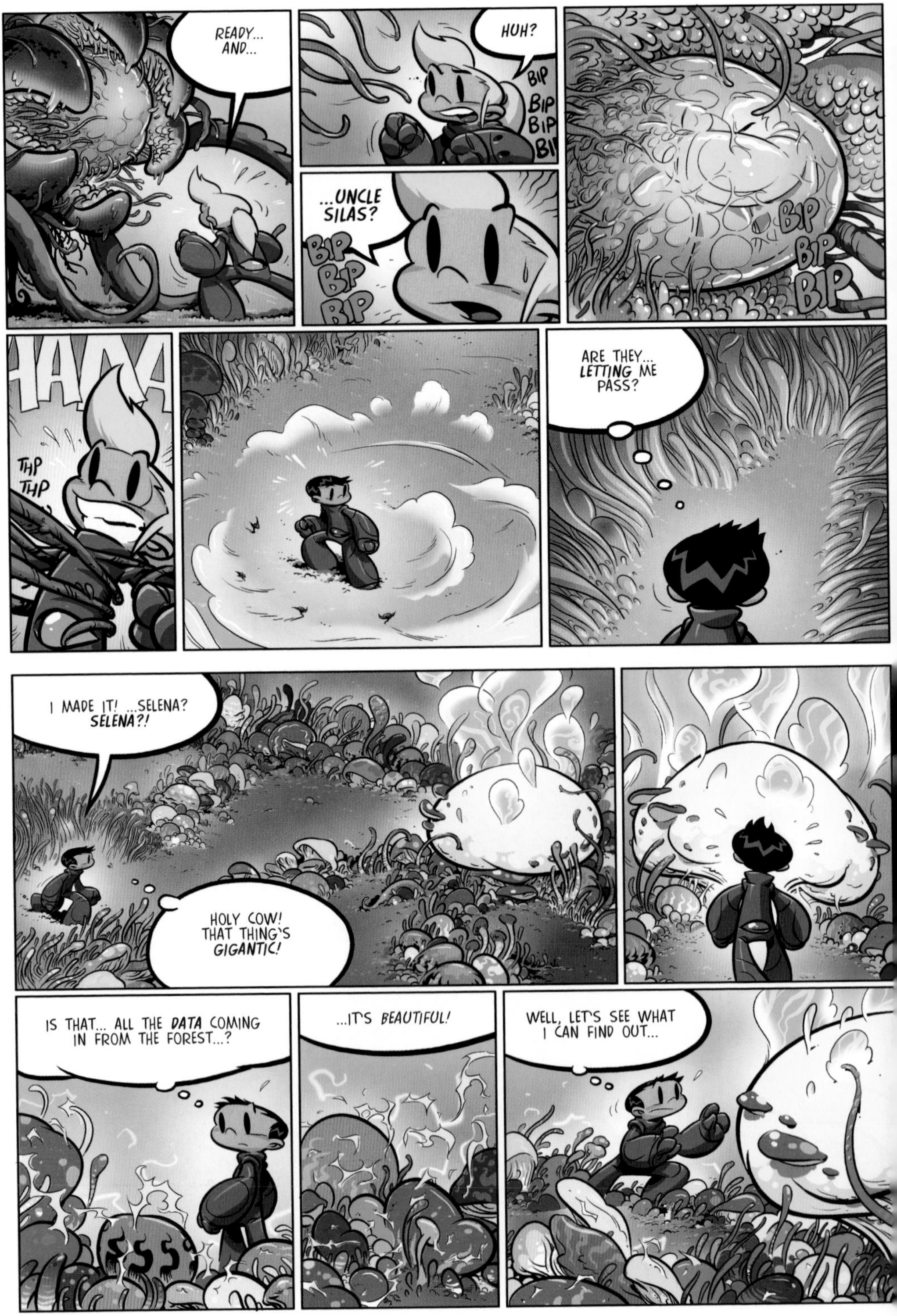
READY... AND...
HUH?
BIP BIP BIP BI
...UNCLE SILAS?
BIP BIP BIP
BIP BIP BIP
THP THP
ARE THEY... LETTING ME PASS?
I MADE IT! ...SELENA? SELENA?!
HOLY COW! THAT THING'S GIGANTIC!
IS THAT... ALL THE DATA COMING IN FROM THE FOREST...?
...IT'S BEAUTIFUL!
WELL, LET'S SEE WHAT I CAN FIND OUT...

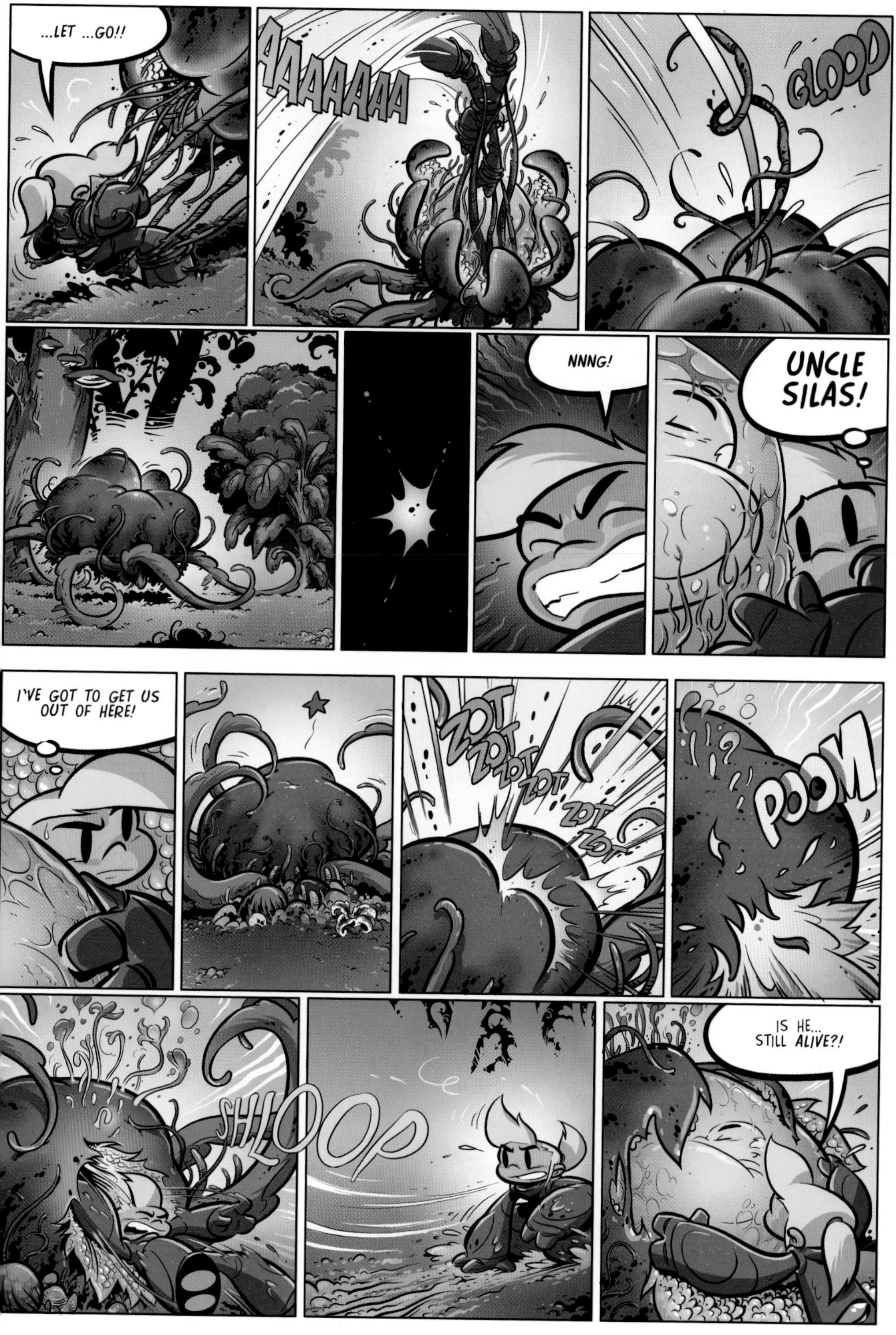
...LET ...GO!!
AAAAAAA
GLOOP
NNNG!
UNCLE SILAS!
I'VE GOT TO GET US OUT OF HERE!
ZOT ZOT ZOT ZOT ZOT ZOT ZOT
POOM
SHLOOP
IS HE... STILL ALIVE?!

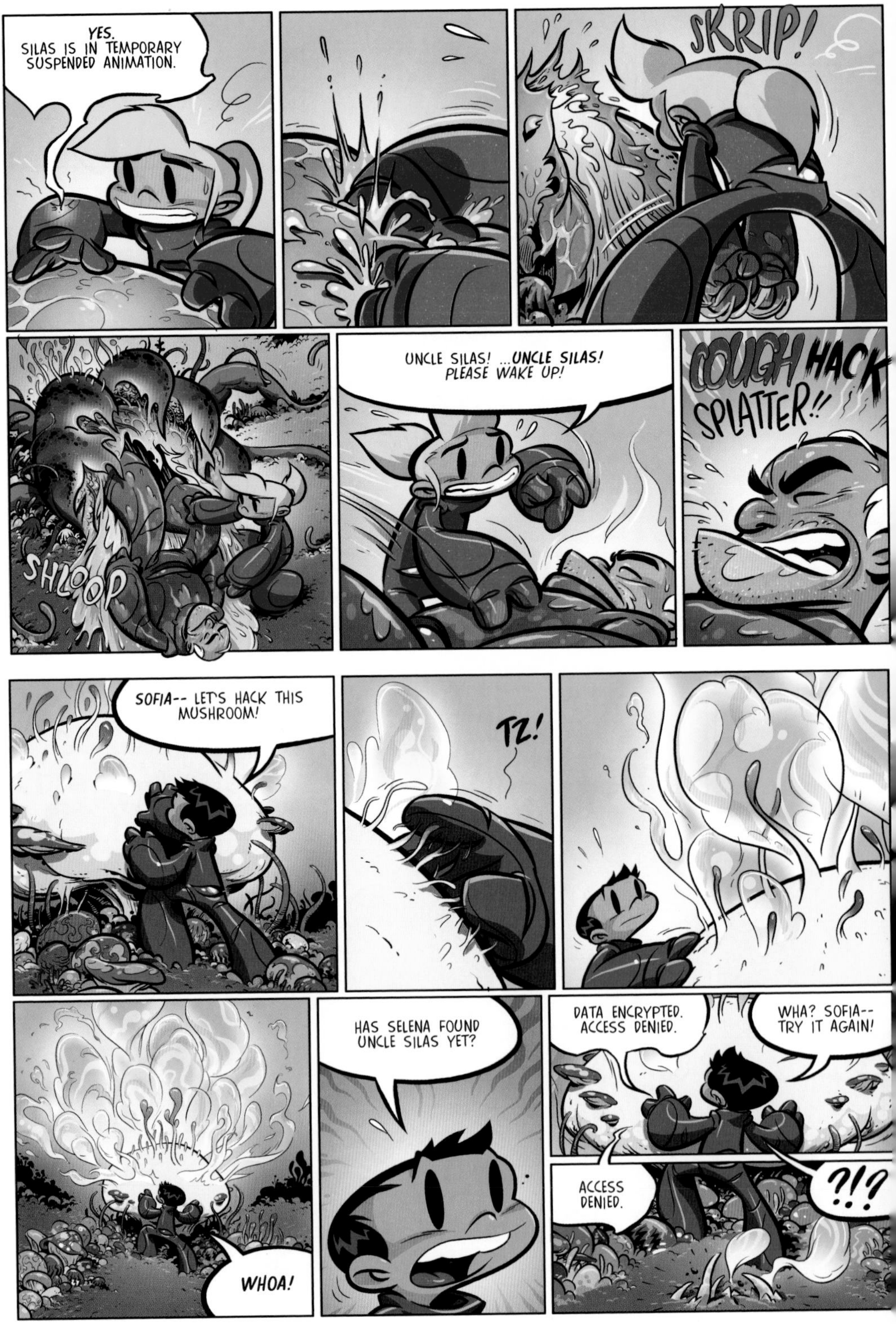
YES. SILAS IS IN TEMPORARY SUSPENDED ANIMATION.
SKRIP!
SHLOOP
UNCLE SILAS! ...UNCLE SILAS! PLEASE WAKE UP!
COUGH HACK
SPLATTER!!
SOFIA-- LET'S HACK THIS MUSHROOM!
TZ!
WHOA!
HAS SELENA FOUND UNCLE SILAS YET?
DATA ENCRYPTED. ACCESS DENIED.
WHA? SOFIA-- TRY IT AGAIN!
ACCESS DENIED.
?!?

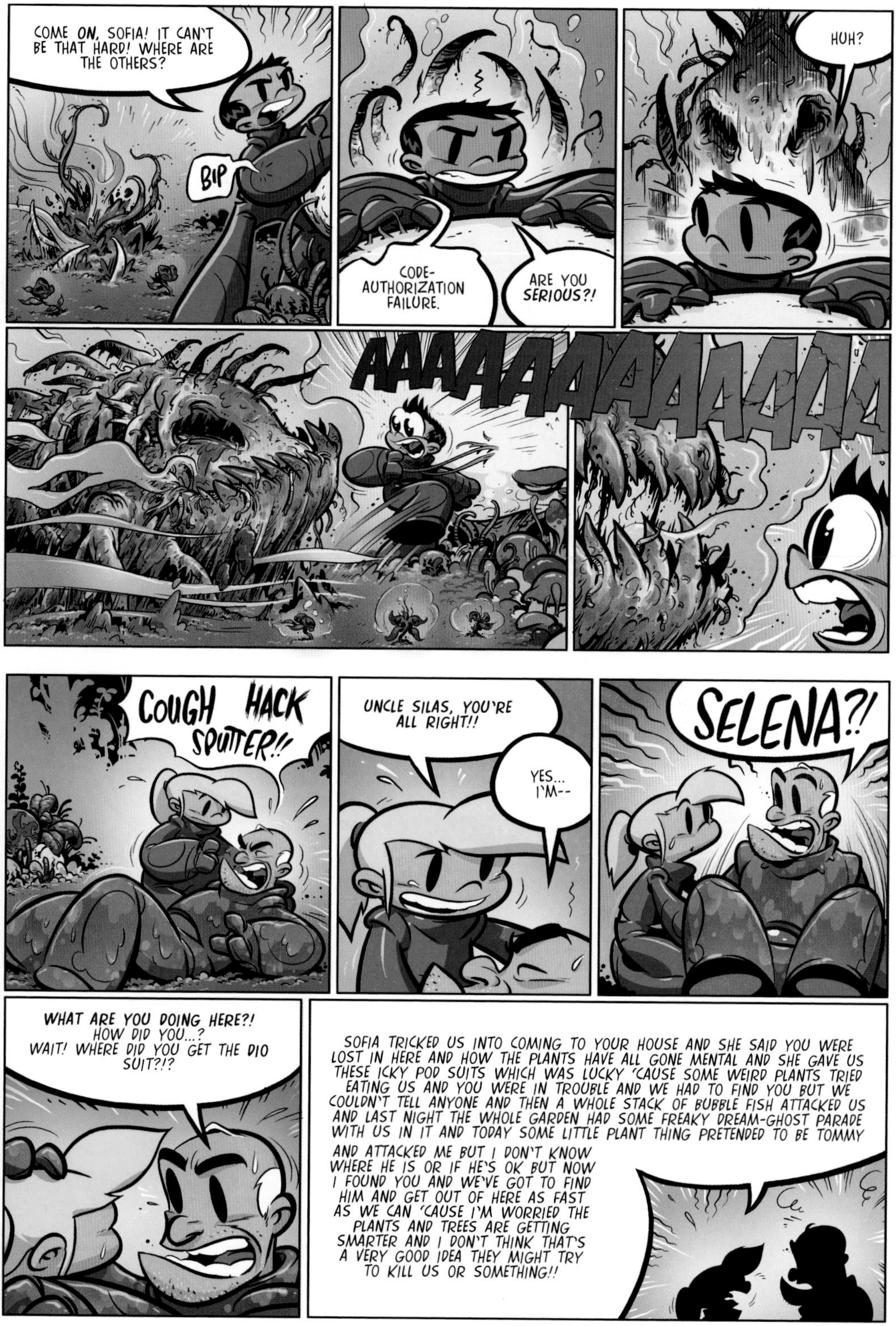
COME ON, SOFIA! IT CAN'T BE THAT HARD! WHERE ARE THE OTHERS?
BIP
CODE-AUTHORIZATION FAILURE.
ARE YOU SERIOUS?!
HUH?
AAAAAAAAAAAAA
COUGH HACK SPUTTER!!
UNCLE SILAS, YOU'RE ALL RIGHT!!
YES... I'M--
SELENA?!
WHAT ARE YOU DOING HERE?! HOW DID YOU...? WAIT! WHERE DID YOU GET THE DIO SUIT?!?
SOFIA TRICKED US INTO COMING TO YOUR HOUSE AND SHE SAID YOU WERE LOST IN HERE AND HOW THE PLANTS HAVE ALL GONE MENTAL AND SHE GAVE US THESE ICKY POD SUITS WHICH WAS LUCKY 'CAUSE SOME WEIRD PLANTS TRIED EATING US AND YOU WERE IN TROUBLE AND WE HAD TO FIND YOU BUT WE COULDN'T TELL ANYONE AND THEN A WHOLE STACK OF BUBBLE FISH ATTACKED US AND LAST NIGHT THE WHOLE GARDEN HAD SOME FREAKY DREAM-GHOST PARADE WITH US IN IT AND TODAY SOME LITTLE PLANT THING PRETENDED TO BE TOMMY AND ATTACKED ME BUT I DON'T KNOW WHERE HE IS OR IF HE'S OK BUT NOW I FOUND YOU AND WE'VE GOT TO FIND HIM AND GET OUT OF HERE AS FAST AS WE CAN 'CAUSE I'M WORRIED THE PLANTS AND TREES ARE GETTING SMARTER AND I DON'T THINK THAT'S A VERY GOOD IDEA THEY MIGHT TRY TO KILL US OR SOMETHING!!

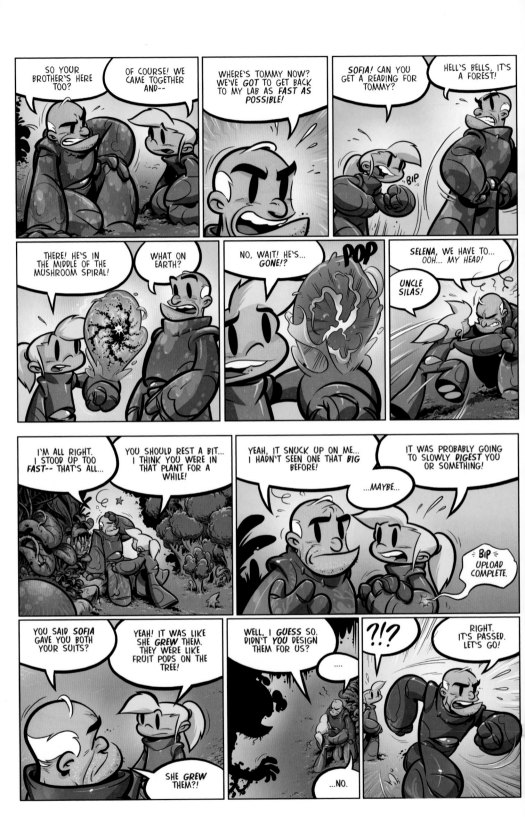

SO YOUR BROTHER'S HERE TOO?

OF COURSE! WE CAME TOGETHER AND--

WHERE'S TOMMY NOW? WE'VE GOT TO GET BACK TO MY LAB AS FAST AS POSSIBLE!

SOFIA! CAN YOU GET A READING FOR TOMMY?

HELL'S BELLS, IT'S A FOREST!

BIP

THERE! HE'S IN THE MIDDLE OF THE MUSHROOM SPIRAL!

WHAT ON EARTH?

NO, WAIT! HE'S... GONE!?

POP

SELENA, WE HAVE TO... OOH... MY HEAD!

UNCLE SILAS!

I'M ALL RIGHT. I STOOD UP TOO FAST-- THAT'S ALL...

YOU SHOULD REST A BIT... I THINK YOU WERE IN THAT PLANT FOR A WHILE!

YEAH, IT SNUCK UP ON ME... I HADN'T SEEN ONE THAT BIG BEFORE!

...MAYBE...

IT WAS PROBABLY GOING TO SLOWLY DIGEST YOU OR SOMETHING!

BIP UPLOAD COMPLETE.

YOU SAID SOFIA GAVE YOU BOTH YOUR SUITS?

YEAH! IT WAS LIKE SHE GREW THEM. THEY WERE LIKE FRUIT PODS ON THE TREE!

WELL, I GUESS SO. DIDN'T YOU DESIGN THEM FOR US?

....

?!?

RIGHT. IT'S PASSED. LET'S GO!

SHE GREW THEM?!

...NO.

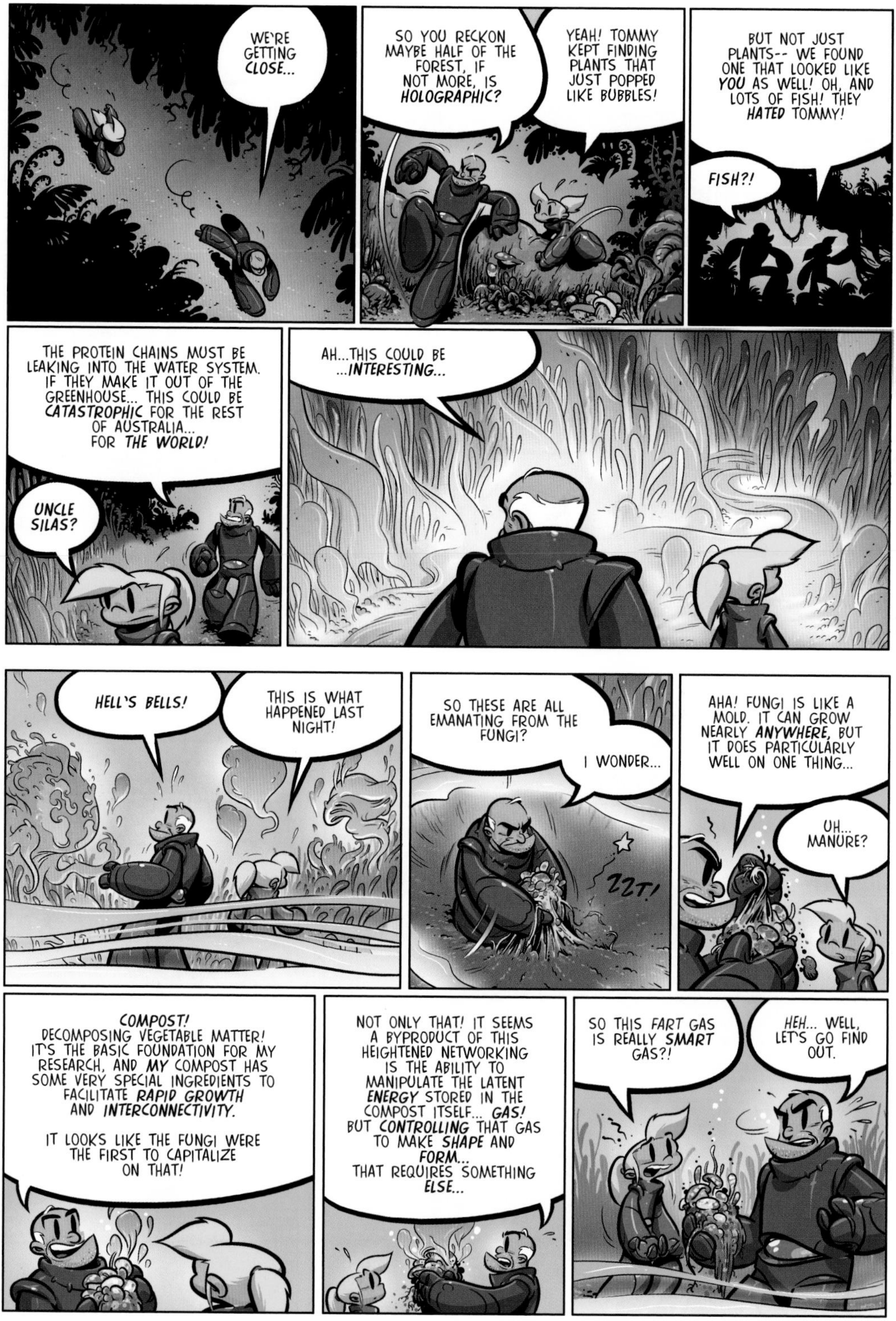

WE'RE GETTING CLOSE...
SO YOU RECKON MAYBE HALF OF THE FOREST, IF NOT MORE, IS HOLOGRAPHIC?
YEAH! TOMMY KEPT FINDING PLANTS THAT JUST POPPED LIKE BUBBLES!
BUT NOT JUST PLANTS-- WE FOUND ONE THAT LOOKED LIKE YOU AS WELL! OH, AND LOTS OF FISH! THEY HATED TOMMY!
FISH?!
THE PROTEIN CHAINS MUST BE LEAKING INTO THE WATER SYSTEM. IF THEY MAKE IT OUT OF THE GREENHOUSE... THIS COULD BE CATASTROPHIC FOR THE REST OF AUSTRALIA... FOR THE WORLD!
UNCLE SILAS?
AH...THIS COULD BE ...INTERESTING...
HELL'S BELLS!
THIS IS WHAT HAPPENED LAST NIGHT!
SO THESE ARE ALL EMANATING FROM THE FUNGI?
I WONDER...
ZZT!
AHA! FUNGI IS LIKE A MOLD. IT CAN GROW NEARLY ANYWHERE, BUT IT DOES PARTICULARLY WELL ON ONE THING...
UH... MANURE?
COMPOST! DECOMPOSING VEGETABLE MATTER! IT'S THE BASIC FOUNDATION FOR MY RESEARCH, AND MY COMPOST HAS SOME VERY SPECIAL INGREDIENTS TO FACILITATE RAPID GROWTH AND INTERCONNECTIVITY.
IT LOOKS LIKE THE FUNGI WERE THE FIRST TO CAPITALIZE ON THAT!
NOT ONLY THAT! IT SEEMS A BYPRODUCT OF THIS HEIGHTENED NETWORKING IS THE ABILITY TO MANIPULATE THE LATENT ENERGY STORED IN THE COMPOST ITSELF... GAS! BUT CONTROLLING THAT GAS TO MAKE SHAPE AND FORM... THAT REQUIRES SOMETHING ELSE...
SO THIS FART GAS IS REALLY SMART GAS?!
HEH... WELL, LET'S GO FIND OUT.

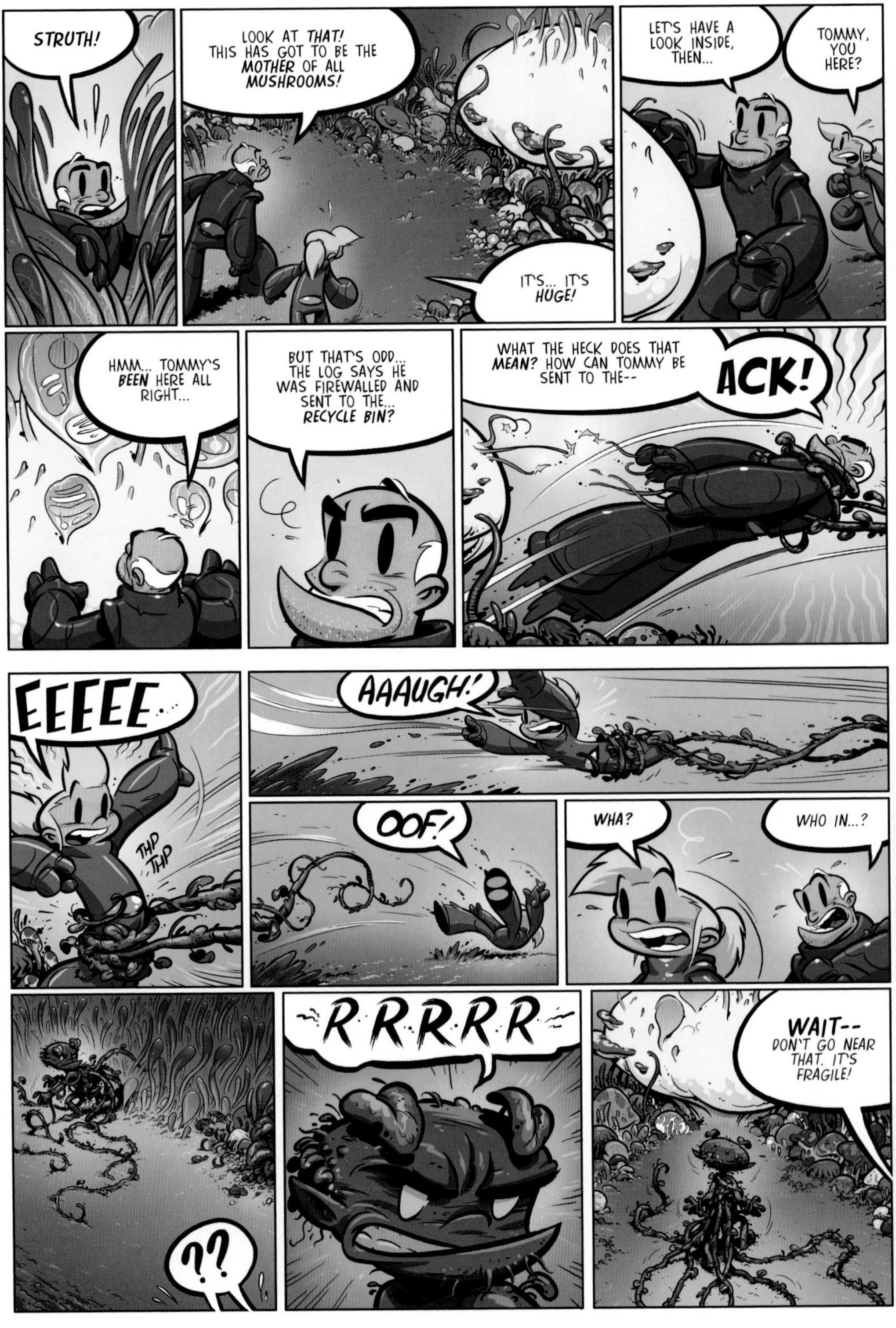
STRUTH!
LOOK AT THAT! THIS HAS GOT TO BE THE MOTHER OF ALL MUSHROOMS!
IT'S... IT'S HUGE!
LET'S HAVE A LOOK INSIDE, THEN...
TOMMY, YOU HERE?
HMM... TOMMY'S BEEN HERE ALL RIGHT...
BUT THAT'S ODD... THE LOG SAYS HE WAS FIREWALLED AND SENT TO THE... RECYCLE BIN?
WHAT THE HECK DOES THAT MEAN? HOW CAN TOMMY BE SENT TO THE--
ACK!
EEEEE
THP THP
AAAUGH!
OOF!
WHA?
WHO IN...?
??
RRRRR
WAIT-- DON'T GO NEAR THAT. IT'S FRAGILE!

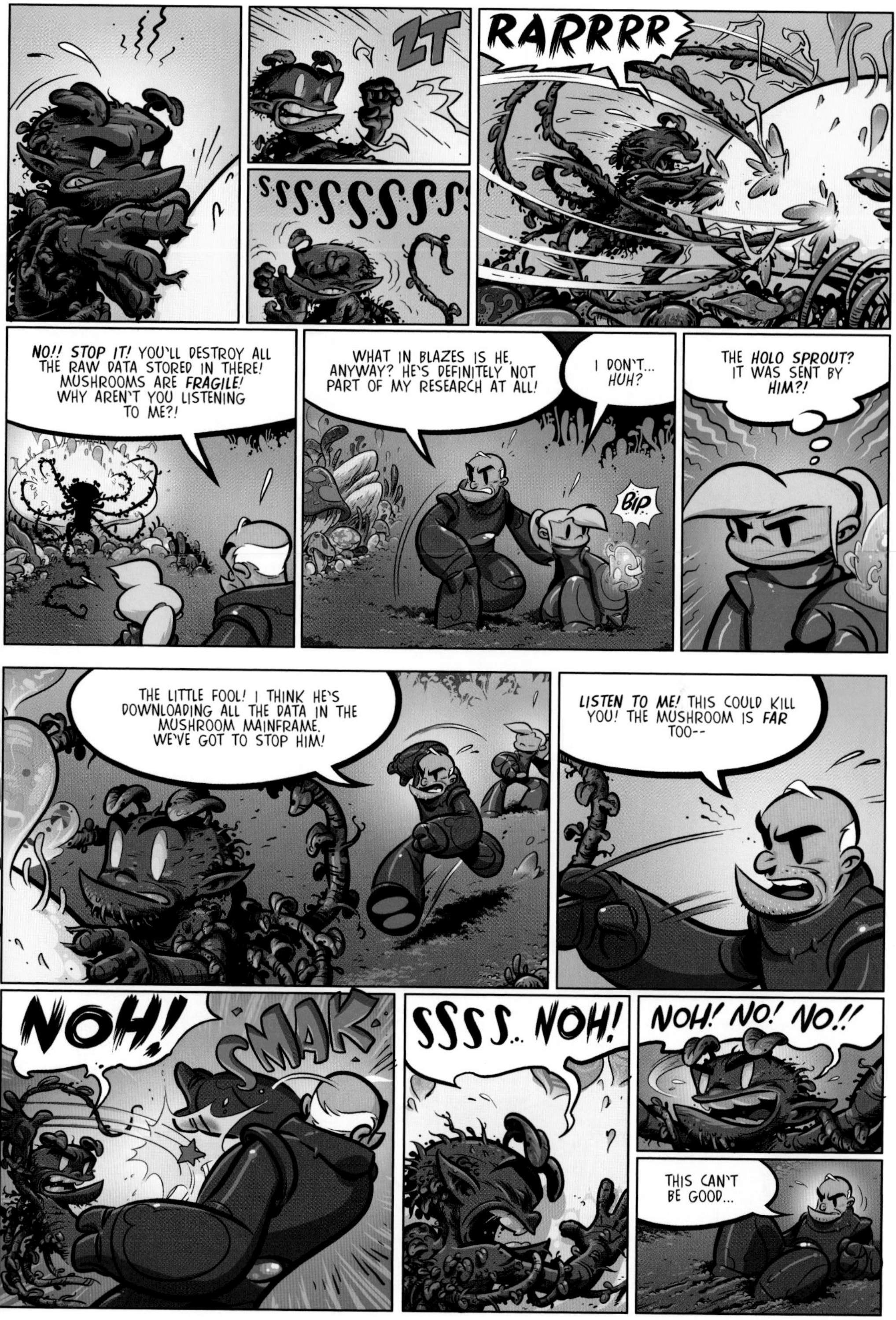
ZT
SSSSSSSSS
RARRRR
NO!! STOP IT! YOU'LL DESTROY ALL THE RAW DATA STORED IN THERE! MUSHROOMS ARE FRAGILE! WHY AREN'T YOU LISTENING TO ME?!
WHAT IN BLAZES IS HE, ANYWAY? HE'S DEFINITELY NOT PART OF MY RESEARCH AT ALL!
I DON'T... HUH?
BIP
THE HOLO SPROUT? IT WAS SENT BY HIM?!
THE LITTLE FOOL! I THINK HE'S DOWNLOADING ALL THE DATA IN THE MUSHROOM MAINFRAME. WE'VE GOT TO STOP HIM!
LISTEN TO ME! THIS COULD KILL YOU! THE MUSHROOM IS FAR TOO--
NOH!
SMAK
SSSS.. NOH!
NOH! NO! NO!!
THIS CAN'T BE GOOD...

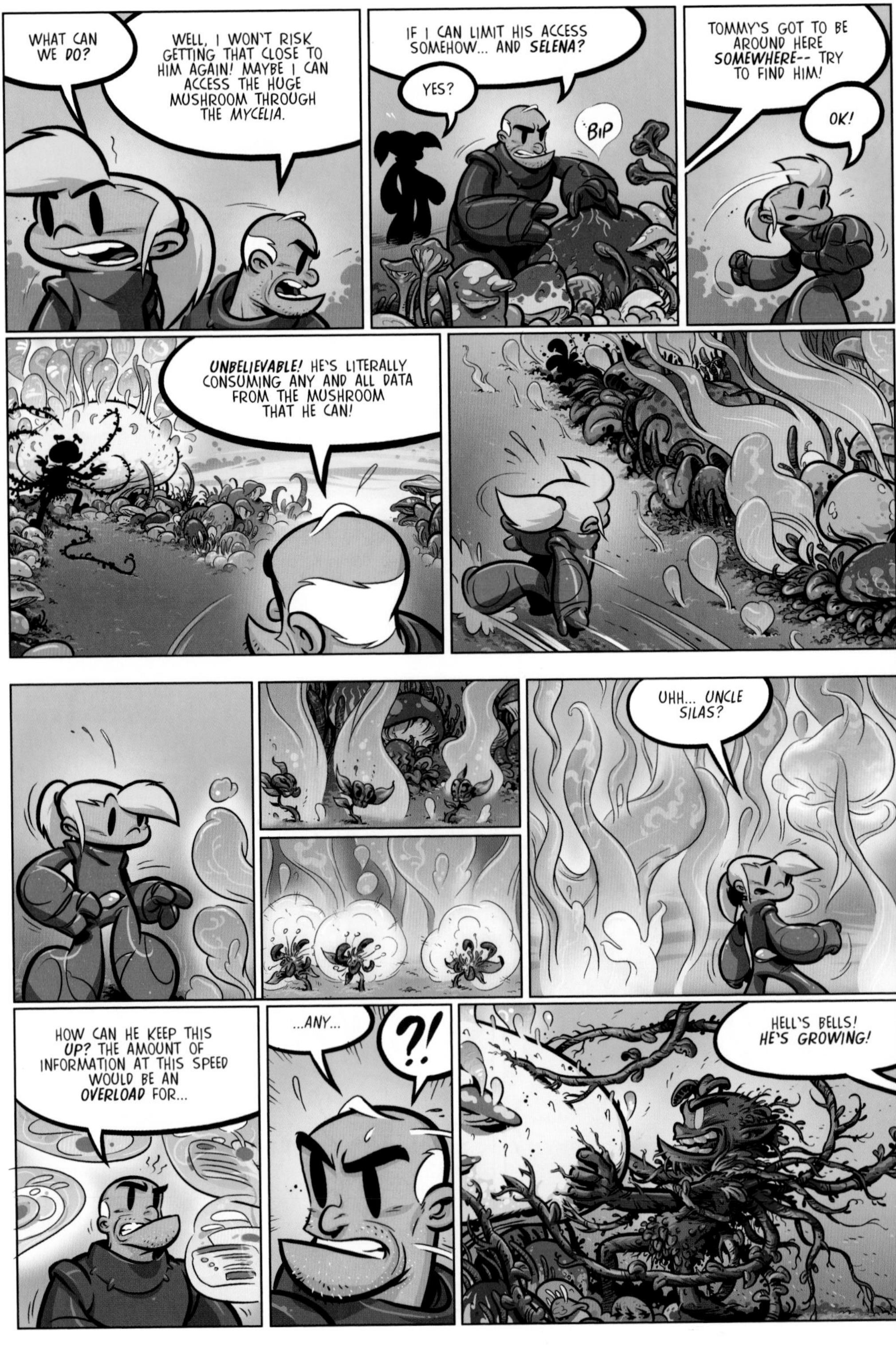
WHAT CAN WE *DO?*
WELL, I WON'T RISK GETTING THAT CLOSE TO HIM AGAIN! MAYBE I CAN ACCESS THE HUGE MUSHROOM THROUGH THE *MYCELIA.*
IF I CAN LIMIT HIS ACCESS SOMEHOW... AND **SELENA?**
YES?
BIP
TOMMY'S GOT TO BE AROUND HERE **SOMEWHERE**-- TRY TO FIND HIM!
OK!
UNBELIEVABLE! HE'S LITERALLY CONSUMING ANY AND ALL DATA FROM THE MUSHROOM THAT HE CAN!
UHH... *UNCLE* SILAS?
HOW CAN HE KEEP THIS **UP?** THE AMOUNT OF INFORMATION AT THIS SPEED WOULD BE AN **OVERLOAD** FOR...
...*ANY*...
?!
HELL'S BELLS! **HE'S GROWING!**

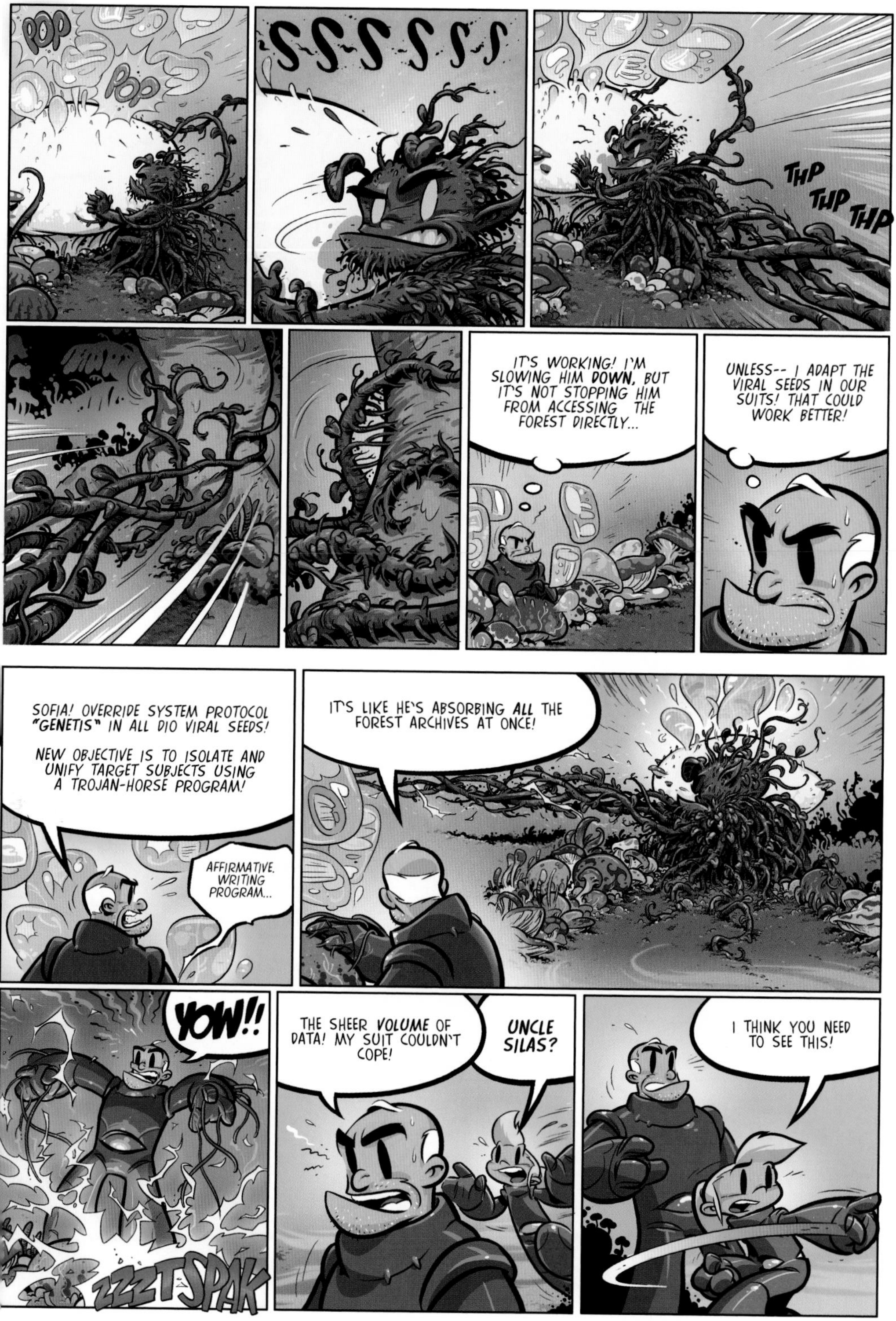
POP
POP
SSSSSS
THP
THP
THP
IT'S WORKING! I'M SLOWING HIM **DOWN**, BUT IT'S NOT STOPPING HIM FROM ACCESSING THE FOREST DIRECTLY...
UNLESS-- I ADAPT THE VIRAL SEEDS IN OUR SUITS! THAT COULD WORK BETTER!
SOFIA! OVERRIDE SYSTEM PROTOCOL **"GENETIS"** IN ALL DIO VIRAL SEEDS!
NEW OBJECTIVE IS TO ISOLATE AND UNIFY TARGET SUBJECTS USING A TROJAN-HORSE PROGRAM!
AFFIRMATIVE. WRITING PROGRAM...
IT'S LIKE HE'S ABSORBING **ALL** THE FOREST ARCHIVES AT ONCE!
YOW!!
ZZZT SPAK
THE SHEER **VOLUME** OF DATA! MY SUIT COULDN'T COPE!
UNCLE SILAS?
I THINK YOU NEED TO SEE THIS!

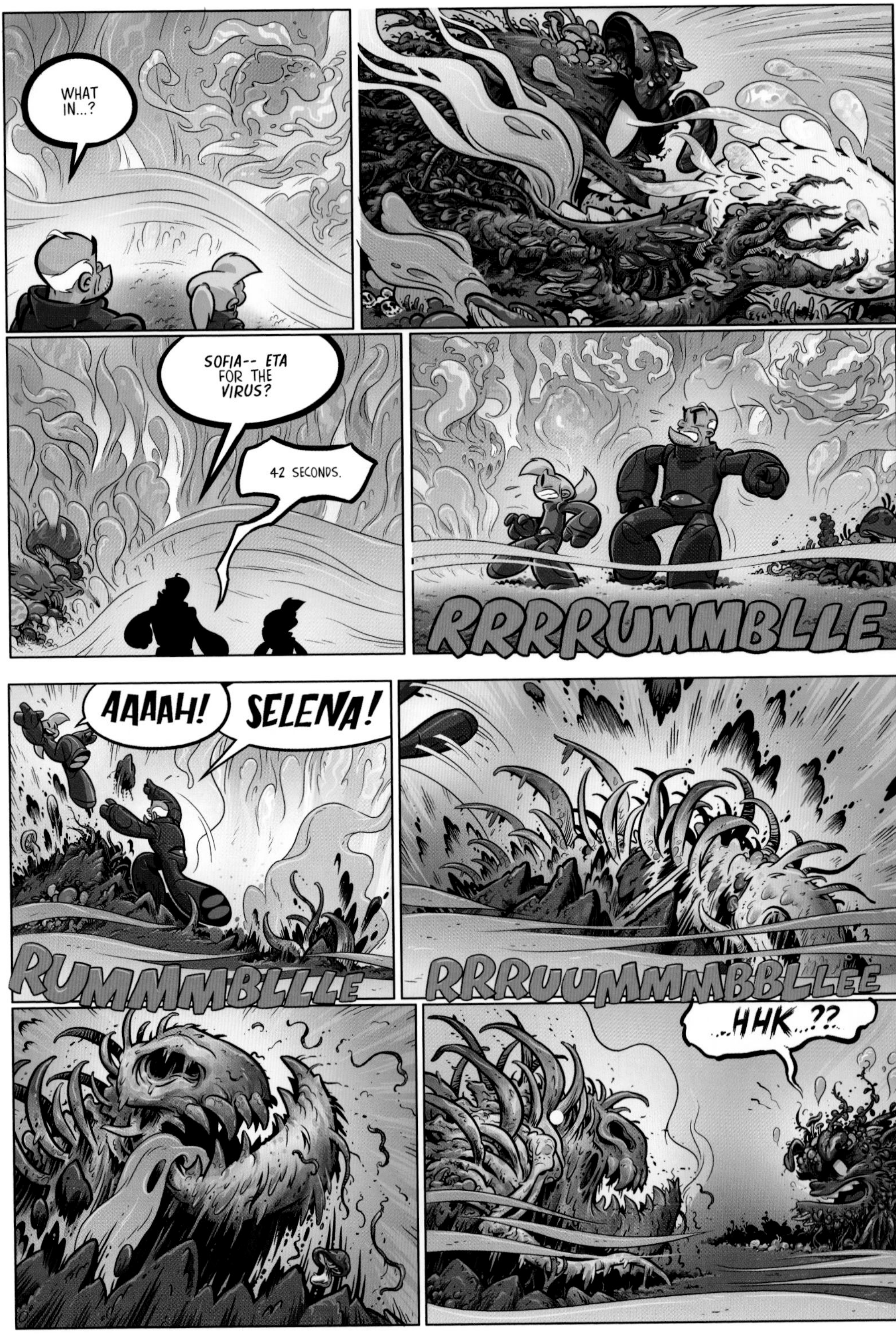
WHAT IN...?
SOFIA-- ETA FOR THE VIRUS?
42 SECONDS.
RRRRUMMBLLE
AAAAH!
SELENA!
RUMMMBLLLE
RRRUUMMMBBLLEE
...HHK...??

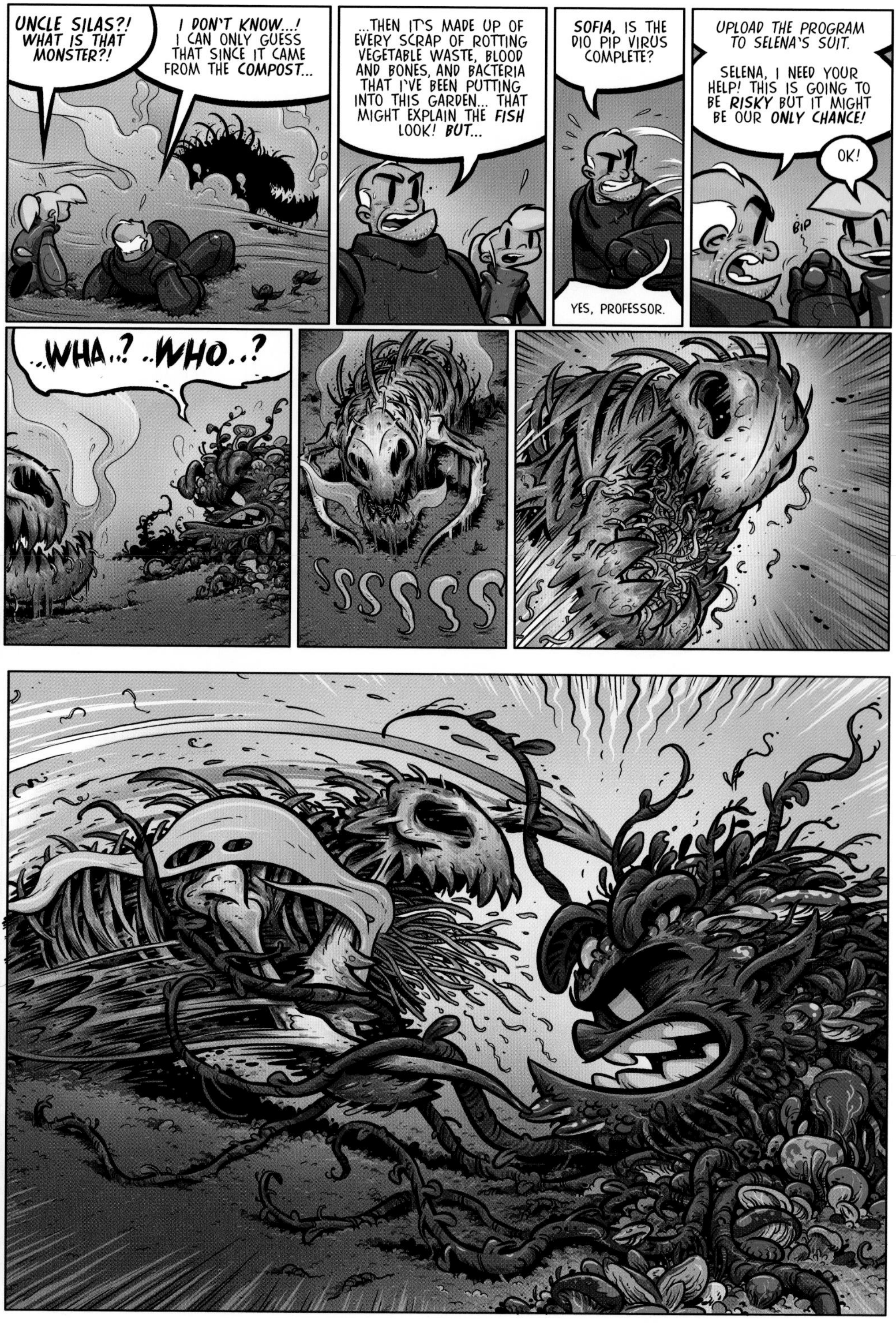
UNCLE SILAS?! WHAT IS THAT MONSTER?!
I DON'T KNOW...! I CAN ONLY GUESS THAT SINCE IT CAME FROM THE COMPOST...
...THEN IT'S MADE UP OF EVERY SCRAP OF ROTTING VEGETABLE WASTE, BLOOD AND BONES, AND BACTERIA THAT I'VE BEEN PUTTING INTO THIS GARDEN... THAT MIGHT EXPLAIN THE FISH LOOK! BUT...
SOFIA, IS THE DIO PIP VIRUS COMPLETE?
YES, PROFESSOR.
UPLOAD THE PROGRAM TO SELENA'S SUIT.
SELENA, I NEED YOUR HELP! THIS IS GOING TO BE RISKY BUT IT MIGHT BE OUR ONLY CHANCE!
OK!
BIP
..WHA..? ..WHO..?
SSSSSS

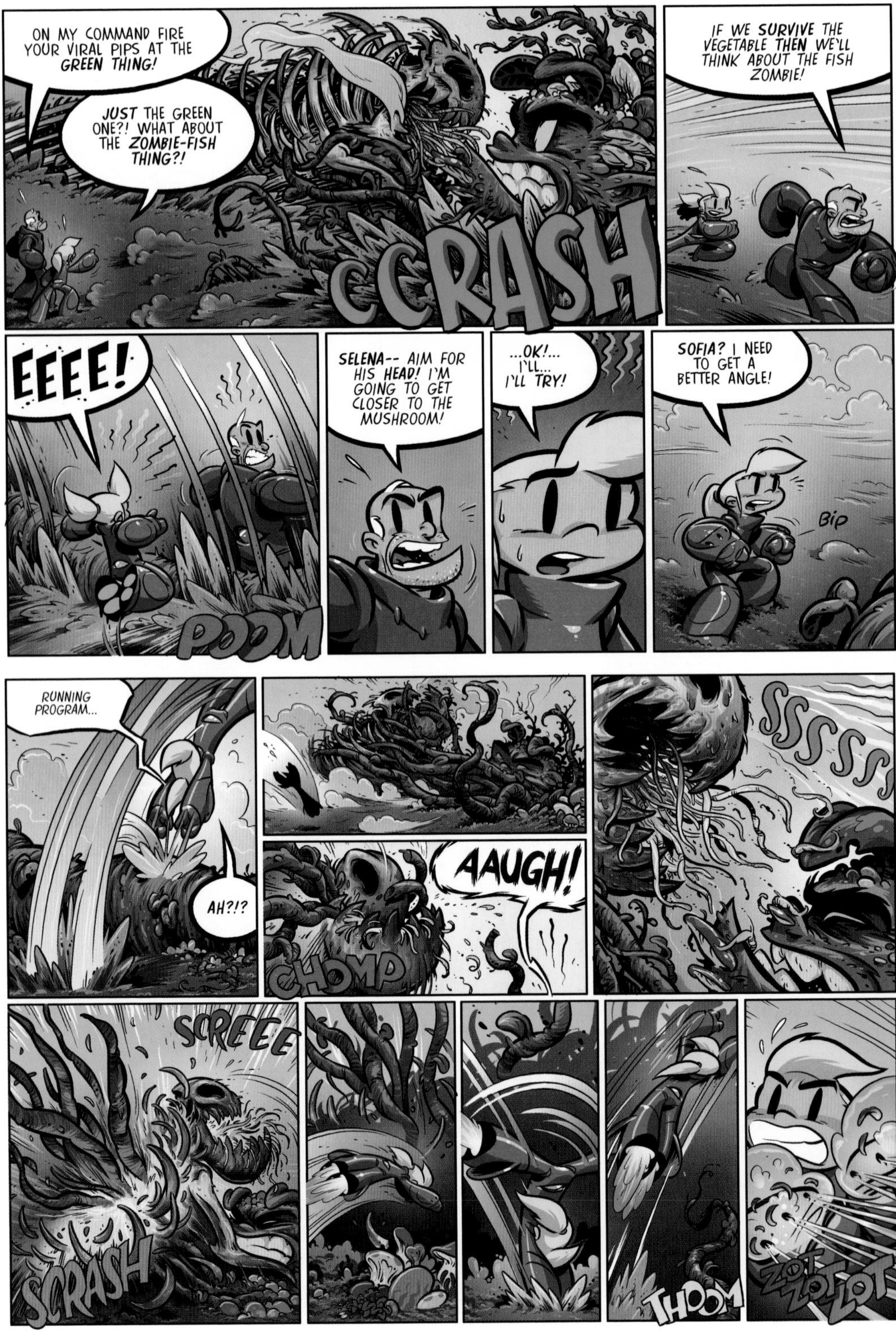
ON MY COMMAND FIRE YOUR VIRAL PIPS AT THE GREEN THING!
JUST THE GREEN ONE?! WHAT ABOUT THE ZOMBIE-FISH THING?!
CCRASH
IF WE SURVIVE THE VEGETABLE THEN WE'LL THINK ABOUT THE FISH ZOMBIE!
EEEE!
POOM
SELENA-- AIM FOR HIS HEAD! I'M GOING TO GET CLOSER TO THE MUSHROOM!
...OK!... I'LL... I'LL TRY!
SOFIA? I NEED TO GET A BETTER ANGLE!
Bip
RUNNING PROGRAM...
AH?!?
AAUGH!
CHOMP
SSSSSS
SCREEEE
SCRASH
THOOM
ZOT ZOT ZOT

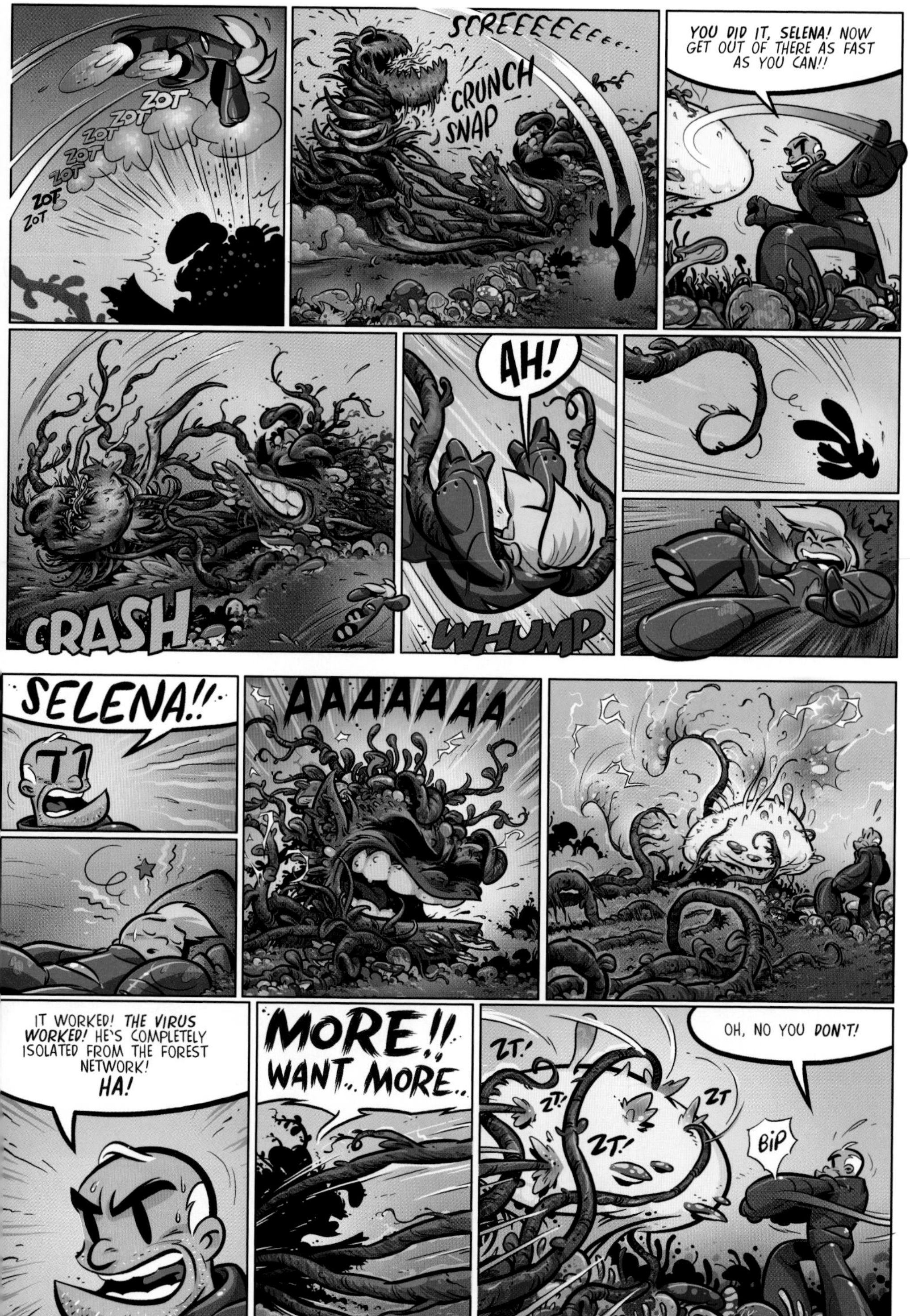
ZOT
ZOT
ZOT
ZOT
ZOT
ZOT
ZOT
SCREEEEEE...
CRUNCH
SNAP
YOU DID IT, SELENA! NOW GET OUT OF THERE AS FAST AS YOU CAN!!
CRASH
AH!
WHUMP
SELENA!!
AAAAAA
IT WORKED! THE VIRUS WORKED! HE'S COMPLETELY ISOLATED FROM THE FOREST NETWORK! HA!
MORE!! WANT.. MORE..
ZT!
ZT!
ZT
ZT!
OH, NO YOU DON'T!
BIP

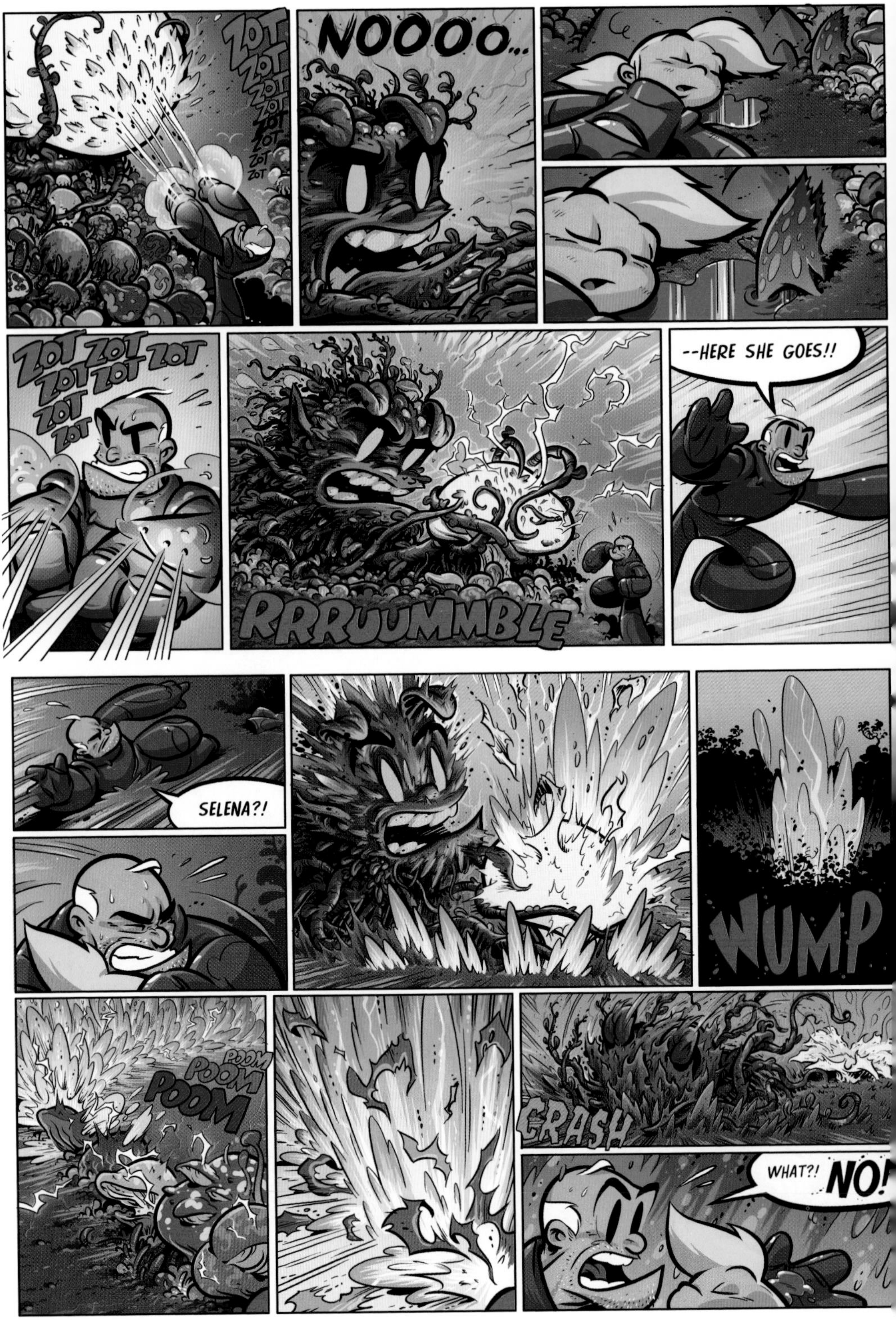
ZOT ZOT ZOT ZOT ZOT ZOT ZOT ZOT
NOOOO...
ZOT ZOT ZOT ZOT ZOT ZOT ZOT
RRRUUMMBLE
--HERE SHE GOES!!
SELENA?!
WUMP
POOM POOM POOM
CRASH
WHAT?! NO!

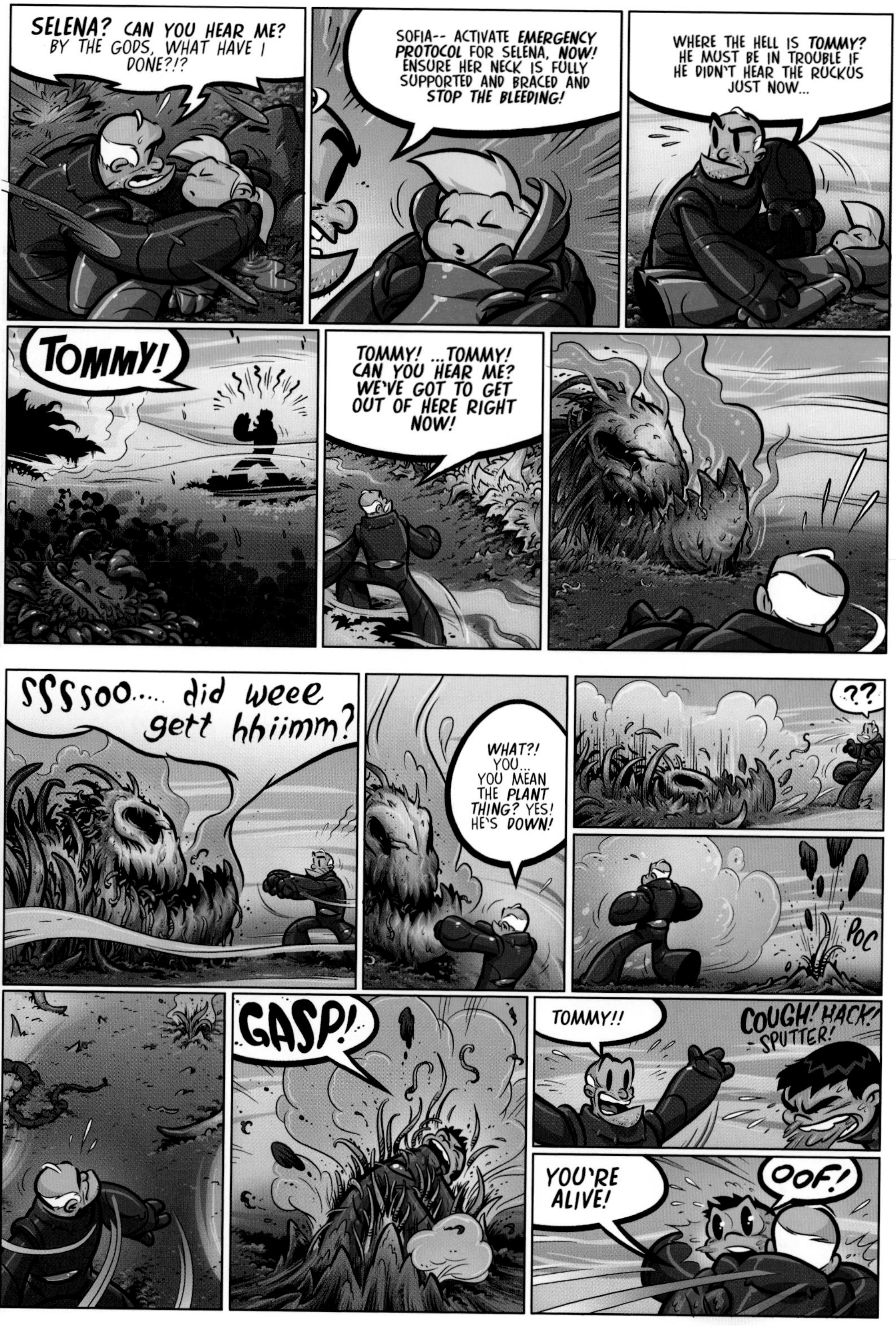
SELENA? CAN YOU HEAR ME? BY THE GODS, WHAT HAVE I DONE?!?
SOFIA-- ACTIVATE EMERGENCY PROTOCOL FOR SELENA, NOW! ENSURE HER NECK IS FULLY SUPPORTED AND BRACED AND STOP THE BLEEDING!
WHERE THE HELL IS TOMMY? HE MUST BE IN TROUBLE IF HE DIDN'T HEAR THE RUCKUS JUST NOW...
TOMMY!
TOMMY! ...TOMMY! CAN YOU HEAR ME? WE'VE GOT TO GET OUT OF HERE RIGHT NOW!
SSSsoo.... did weee gett hhiimm?
WHAT?! YOU... YOU MEAN THE PLANT THING? YES! HE'S DOWN!
??
POC
GASP!
TOMMY!!
COUGH! HACK! SPUTTER!
YOU'RE ALIVE!
OOF!

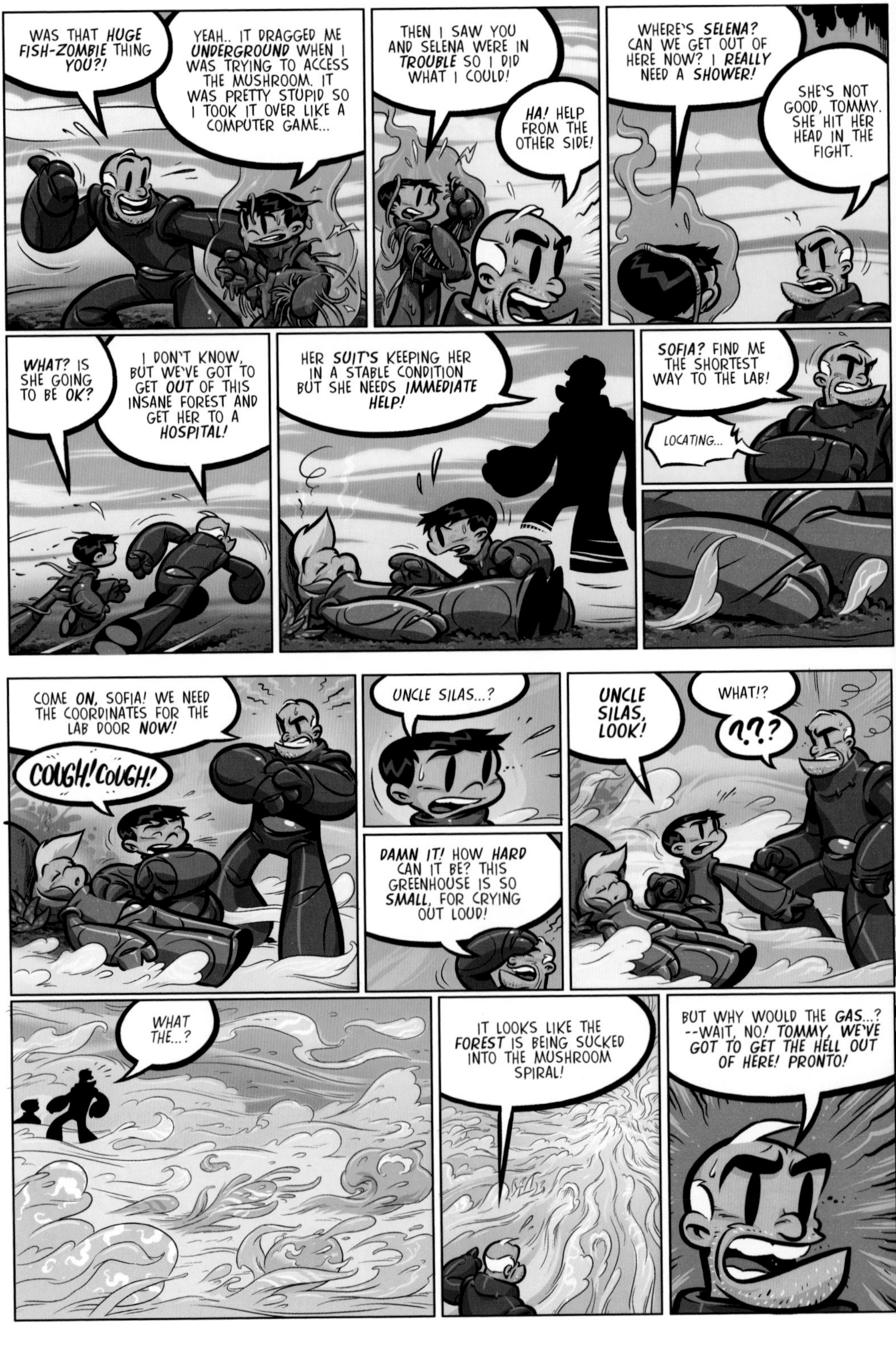
WAS THAT HUGE FISH-ZOMBIE THING YOU?!
YEAH.. IT DRAGGED ME UNDERGROUND WHEN I WAS TRYING TO ACCESS THE MUSHROOM. IT WAS PRETTY STUPID SO I TOOK IT OVER LIKE A COMPUTER GAME...
THEN I SAW YOU AND SELENA WERE IN TROUBLE SO I DID WHAT I COULD!
HA! HELP FROM THE OTHER SIDE!
WHERE'S SELENA? CAN WE GET OUT OF HERE NOW? I REALLY NEED A SHOWER!
SHE'S NOT GOOD, TOMMY. SHE HIT HER HEAD IN THE FIGHT.
WHAT? IS SHE GOING TO BE OK?
I DON'T KNOW, BUT WE'VE GOT TO GET OUT OF THIS INSANE FOREST AND GET HER TO A HOSPITAL!
HER SUIT'S KEEPING HER IN A STABLE CONDITION BUT SHE NEEDS IMMEDIATE HELP!
SOFIA? FIND ME THE SHORTEST WAY TO THE LAB!
LOCATING...
COME ON, SOFIA! WE NEED THE COORDINATES FOR THE LAB DOOR NOW!
COUGH! COUGH!
UNCLE SILAS...?
DAMN IT! HOW HARD CAN IT BE? THIS GREENHOUSE IS SO SMALL, FOR CRYING OUT LOUD!
UNCLE SILAS, LOOK!
WHAT!?
???
WHAT THE...?
IT LOOKS LIKE THE FOREST IS BEING SUCKED INTO THE MUSHROOM SPIRAL!
BUT WHY WOULD THE GAS...? --WAIT, NO! TOMMY, WE'VE GOT TO GET THE HELL OUT OF HERE! PRONTO!

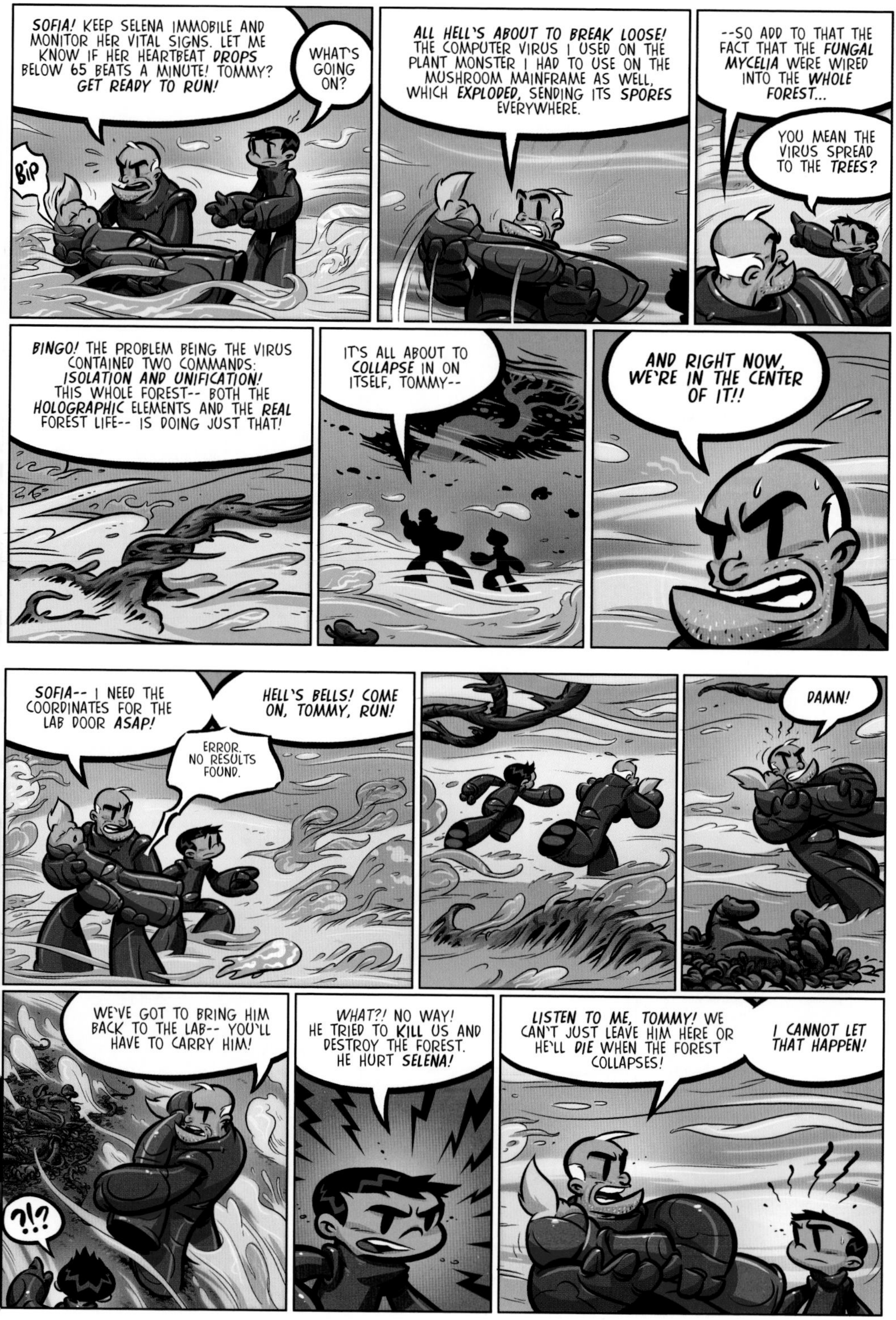
SOFIA! KEEP SELENA IMMOBILE AND MONITOR HER VITAL SIGNS. LET ME KNOW IF HER HEARTBEAT DROPS BELOW 65 BEATS A MINUTE! TOMMY? GET READY TO RUN!
BIP
WHAT'S GOING ON?
ALL HELL'S ABOUT TO BREAK LOOSE! THE COMPUTER VIRUS I USED ON THE PLANT MONSTER I HAD TO USE ON THE MUSHROOM MAINFRAME AS WELL, WHICH EXPLODED, SENDING ITS SPORES EVERYWHERE.
--SO ADD TO THAT THE FACT THAT THE FUNGAL MYCELIA WERE WIRED INTO THE WHOLE FOREST...
YOU MEAN THE VIRUS SPREAD TO THE TREES?
BINGO! THE PROBLEM BEING THE VIRUS CONTAINED TWO COMMANDS: ISOLATION AND UNIFICATION! THIS WHOLE FOREST-- BOTH THE HOLOGRAPHIC ELEMENTS AND THE REAL FOREST LIFE-- IS DOING JUST THAT!
IT'S ALL ABOUT TO COLLAPSE IN ON ITSELF, TOMMY--
AND RIGHT NOW, WE'RE IN THE CENTER OF IT!!
SOFIA-- I NEED THE COORDINATES FOR THE LAB DOOR ASAP!
HELL'S BELLS! COME ON, TOMMY, RUN!
ERROR. NO RESULTS FOUND.
DAMN!
WE'VE GOT TO BRING HIM BACK TO THE LAB-- YOU'LL HAVE TO CARRY HIM!
?!?
WHAT?! NO WAY! HE TRIED TO KILL US AND DESTROY THE FOREST. HE HURT SELENA!
LISTEN TO ME, TOMMY! WE CAN'T JUST LEAVE HIM HERE OR HE'LL DIE WHEN THE FOREST COLLAPSES!
I CANNOT LET THAT HAPPEN!

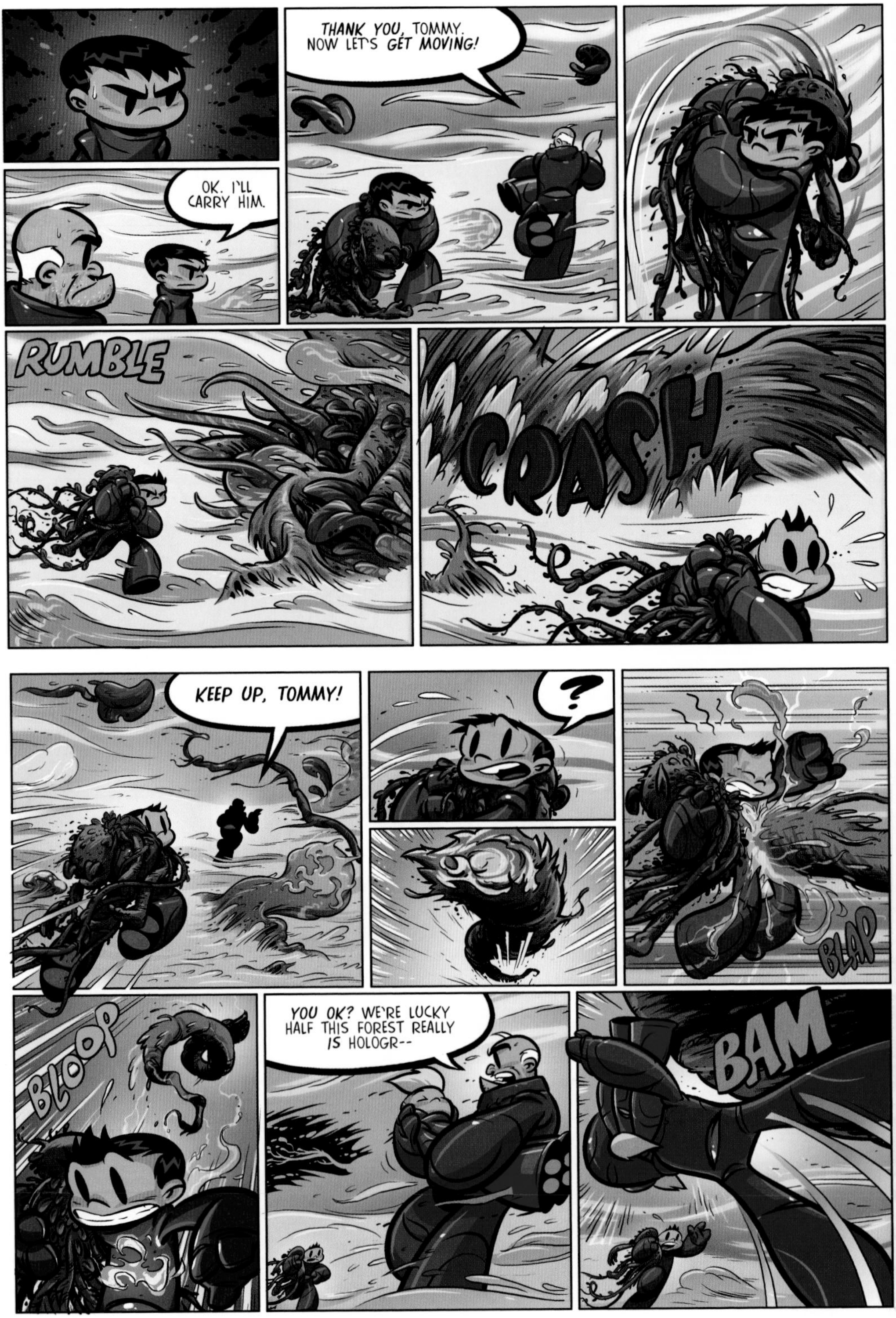
THANK YOU, TOMMY. NOW LET'S GET MOVING!
OK. I'LL CARRY HIM.
RUMBLE
CRASH
KEEP UP, TOMMY!
?
BLAP
BLOOP
YOU OK? WE'RE LUCKY HALF THIS FOREST REALLY IS HOLOGR--
BAM

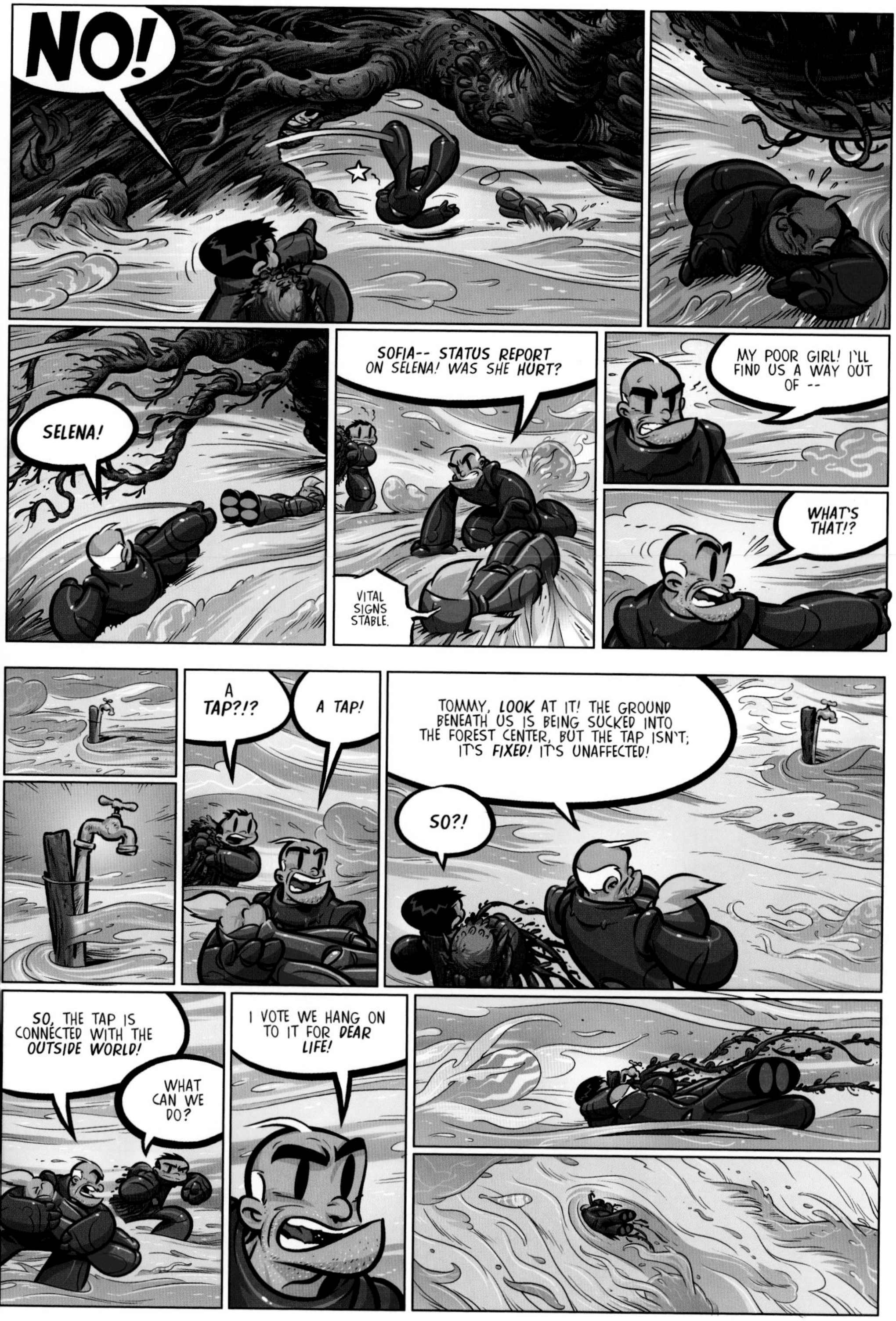
NO!
SELENA!
SOFIA-- STATUS REPORT ON SELENA! WAS SHE HURT?
VITAL SIGNS STABLE.
MY POOR GIRL! I'LL FIND US A WAY OUT OF --
WHAT'S THAT!?
A TAP?!?
A TAP!
TOMMY, LOOK AT IT! THE GROUND BENEATH US IS BEING SUCKED INTO THE FOREST CENTER, BUT THE TAP ISN'T; IT'S FIXED! IT'S UNAFFECTED!
SO?!
SO, THE TAP IS CONNECTED WITH THE OUTSIDE WORLD!
WHAT CAN WE DO?
I VOTE WE HANG ON TO IT FOR DEAR LIFE!

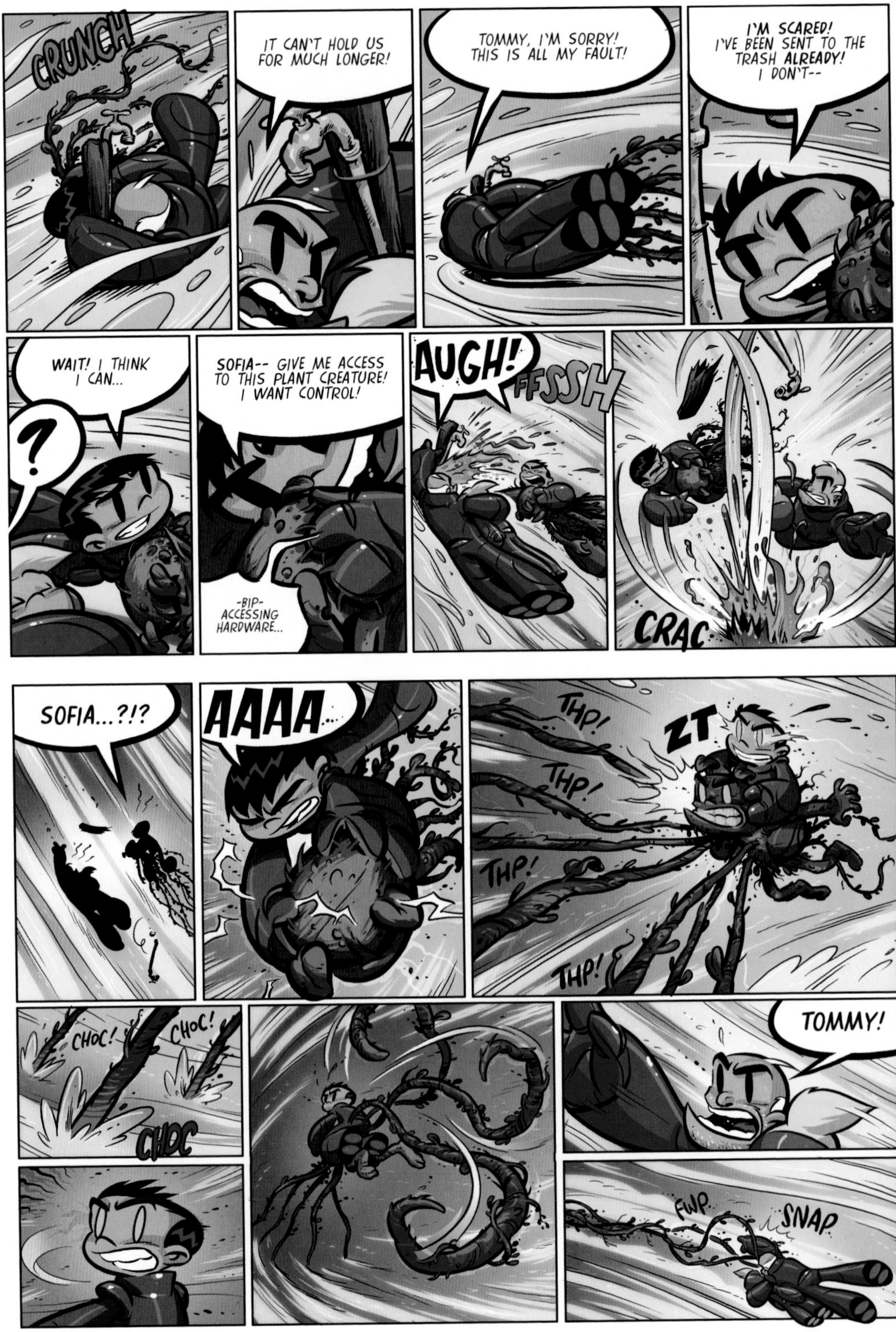
CRUNCH
IT CAN'T HOLD US FOR MUCH LONGER!
TOMMY, I'M SORRY! THIS IS ALL MY FAULT!
I'M SCARED! I'VE BEEN SENT TO THE TRASH ALREADY! I DON'T--
WAIT! I THINK I CAN...
?
SOFIA-- GIVE ME ACCESS TO THIS PLANT CREATURE! I WANT CONTROL!
-BIP- ACCESSING HARDWARE...
AUGH!
FFSSH
CRAC
SOFIA...?!?
AAAA...
THP!
ZT
THP!
THP!
THP!
CHOC!
CHOC!
CHOC
TOMMY!
FWP..
SNAP

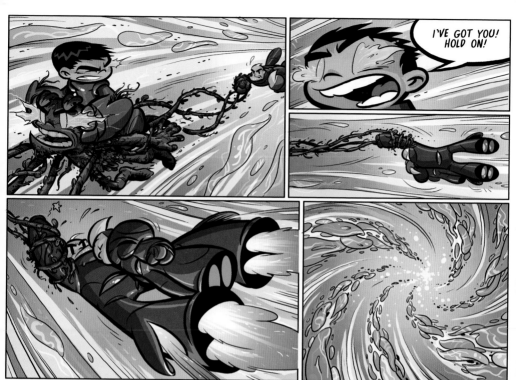

I'VE GOT YOU!
HOLD ON!

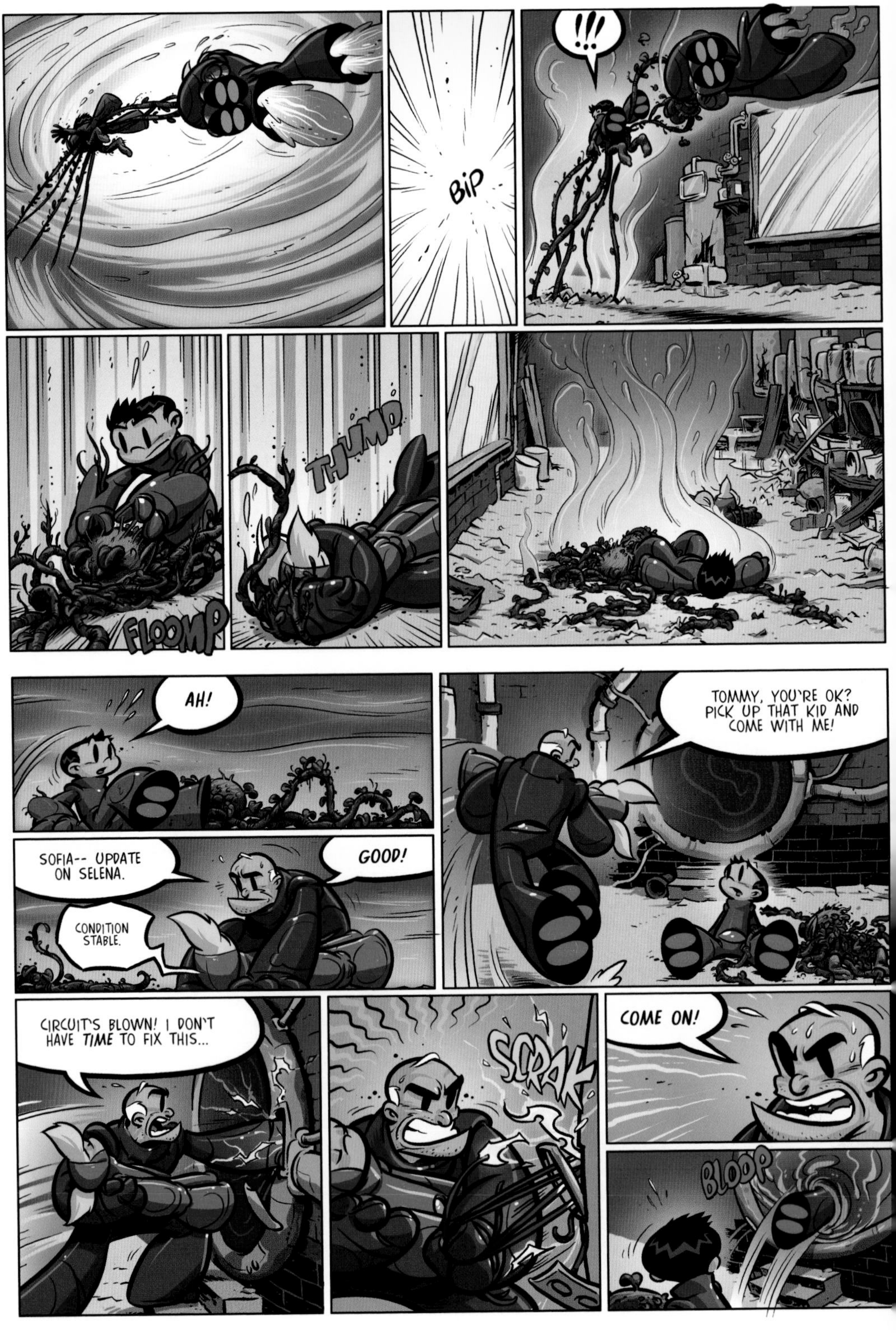
BIP
!!!
THUMP
FLOOMP
AH!
TOMMY, YOU'RE OK? PICK UP THAT KID AND COME WITH ME!
SOFIA-- UPDATE ON SELENA.
CONDITION STABLE.
GOOD!
CIRCUIT'S BLOWN! I DON'T HAVE *TIME* TO FIX THIS...
SCRAK
COME ON!
BLOOP

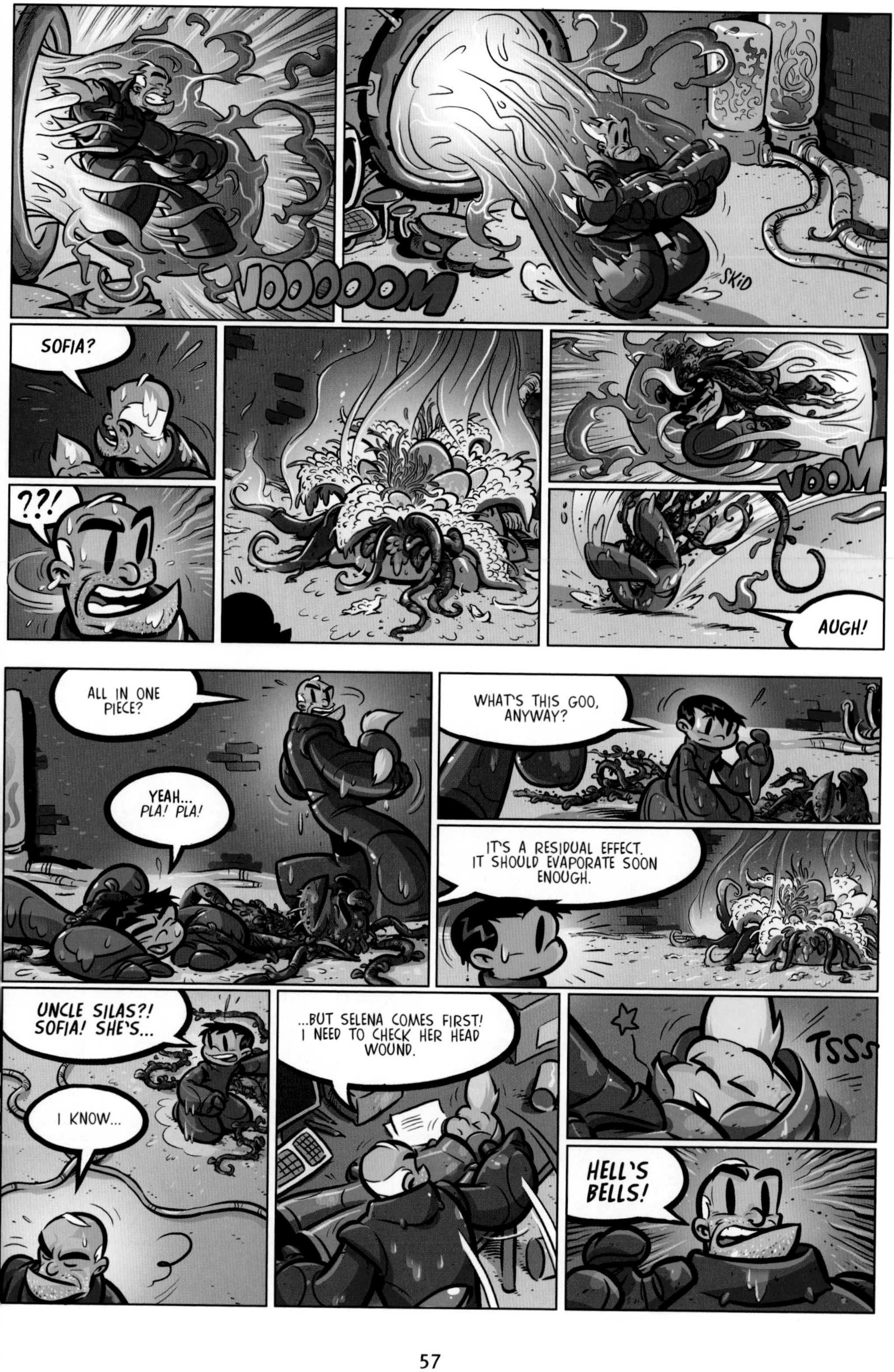
VOOOOOM
SKID
SOFIA?
??!
VOOM
AUGH!
ALL IN ONE PIECE?
YEAH... PLA! PLA!
WHAT'S THIS GOO, ANYWAY?
IT'S A RESIDUAL EFFECT. IT SHOULD EVAPORATE SOON ENOUGH.
UNCLE SILAS?! SOFIA! SHE'S...
I KNOW...
...BUT SELENA COMES FIRST! I NEED TO CHECK HER HEAD WOUND.
TSSS
HELL'S BELLS!

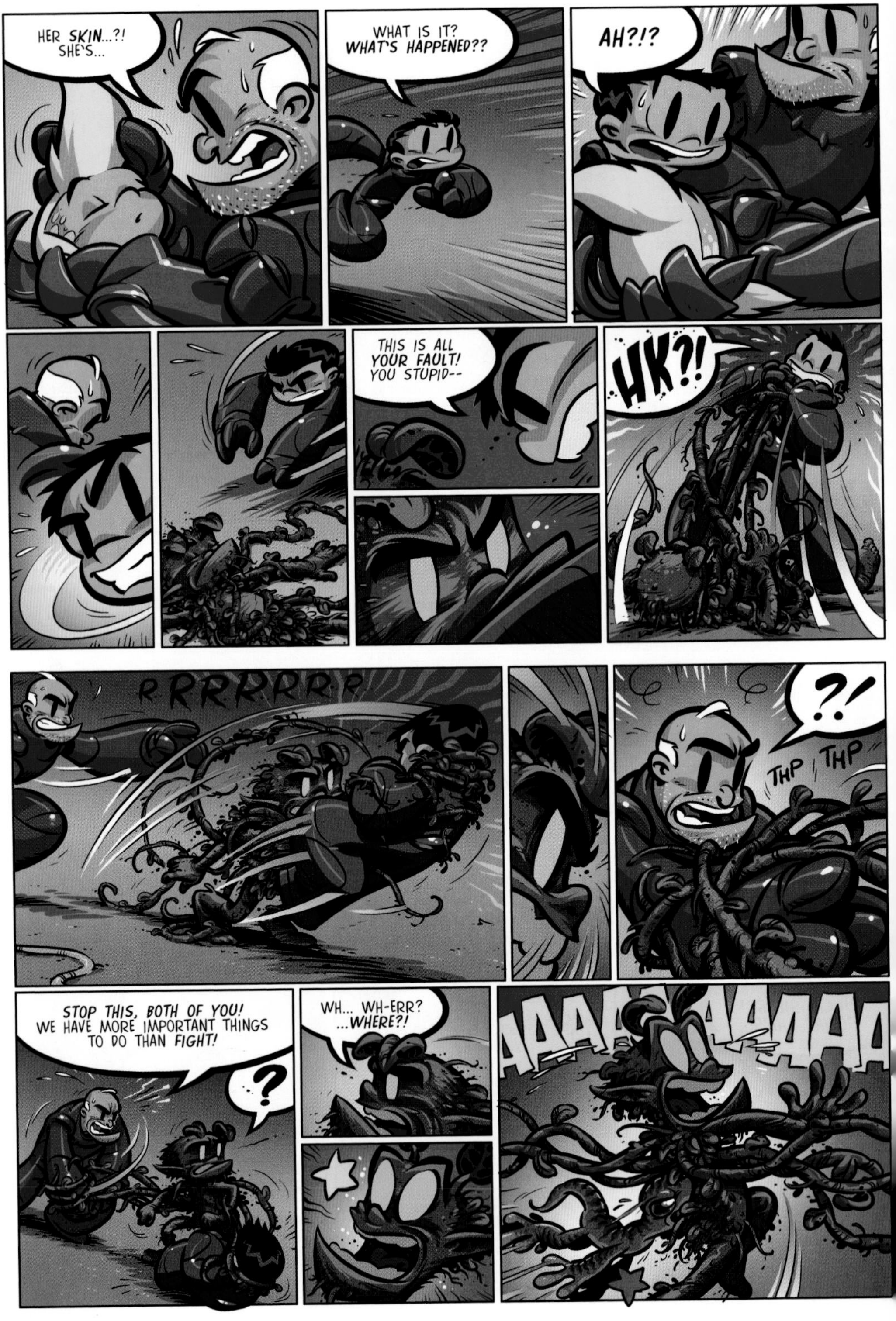
HER SKIN...?! SHE'S...
WHAT IS IT? WHAT'S HAPPENED??
AH?!?
THIS IS ALL YOUR FAULT! YOU STUPID--
HK?!
RRRRRRRR
?!
THP THP
STOP THIS, BOTH OF YOU! WE HAVE MORE IMPORTANT THINGS TO DO THAN FIGHT!
?
WH... WH-ERR? ...WHERE?!

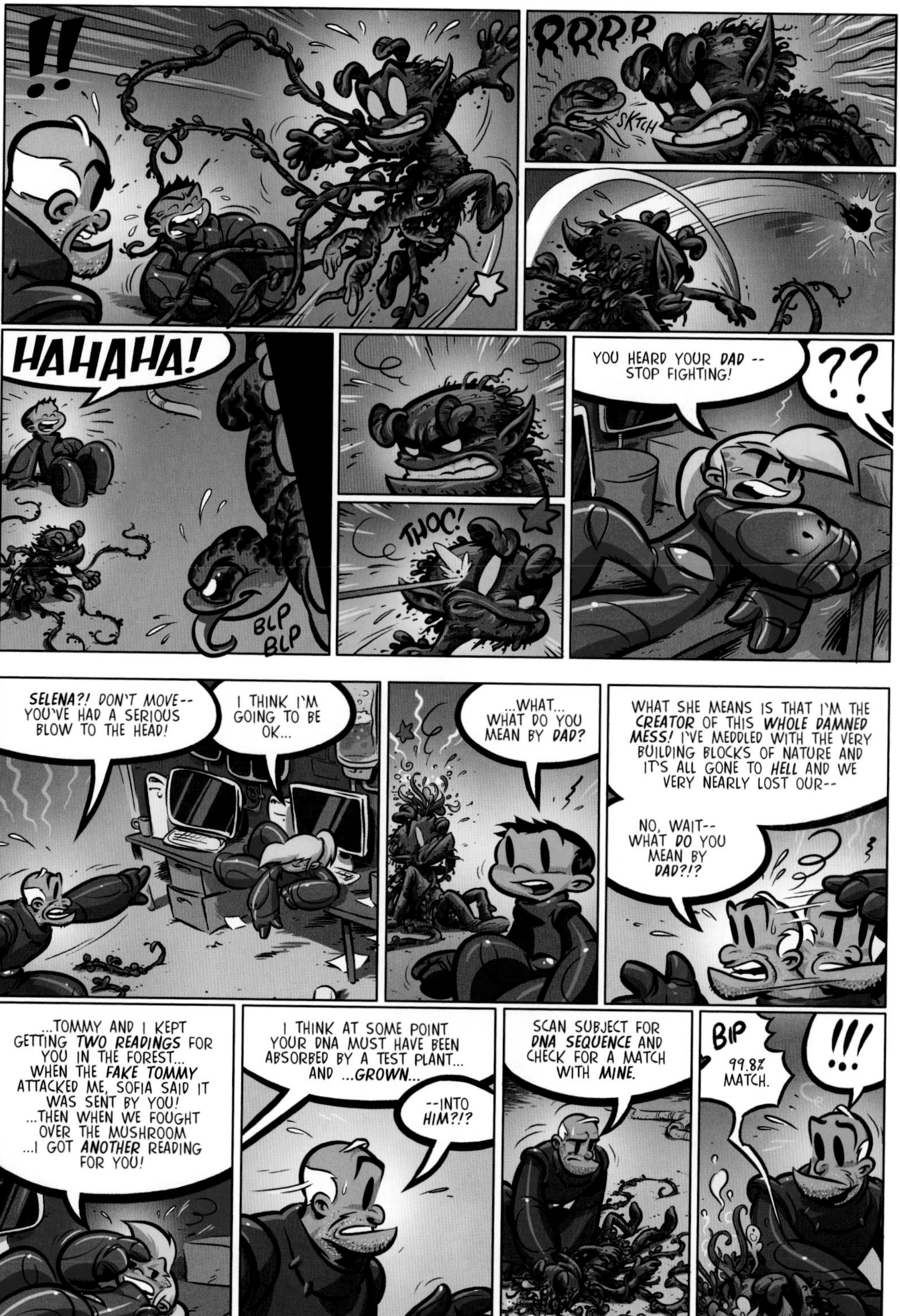
!!
RRRR
SKTCH
HAHAHA!
BLP BLP
THOC!
YOU HEARD YOUR DAD -- STOP FIGHTING!
??
SELENA?! DON'T MOVE-- YOU'VE HAD A SERIOUS BLOW TO THE HEAD!
I THINK I'M GOING TO BE OK...
...WHAT... WHAT DO YOU MEAN BY DAD?
WHAT SHE MEANS IS THAT I'M THE CREATOR OF THIS WHOLE DAMNED MESS! I'VE MEDDLED WITH THE VERY BUILDING BLOCKS OF NATURE AND IT'S ALL GONE TO HELL AND WE VERY NEARLY LOST OUR--
NO, WAIT-- WHAT DO YOU MEAN BY DAD?!?
...TOMMY AND I KEPT GETTING TWO READINGS FOR YOU IN THE FOREST... WHEN THE FAKE TOMMY ATTACKED ME, SOFIA SAID IT WAS SENT BY YOU! ...THEN WHEN WE FOUGHT OVER THE MUSHROOM ...I GOT ANOTHER READING FOR YOU!
I THINK AT SOME POINT YOUR DNA MUST HAVE BEEN ABSORBED BY A TEST PLANT... AND ...GROWN...
--INTO HIM?!?
SCAN SUBJECT FOR DNA SEQUENCE AND CHECK FOR A MATCH WITH MINE.
BIP
99.8% MATCH.
!!!

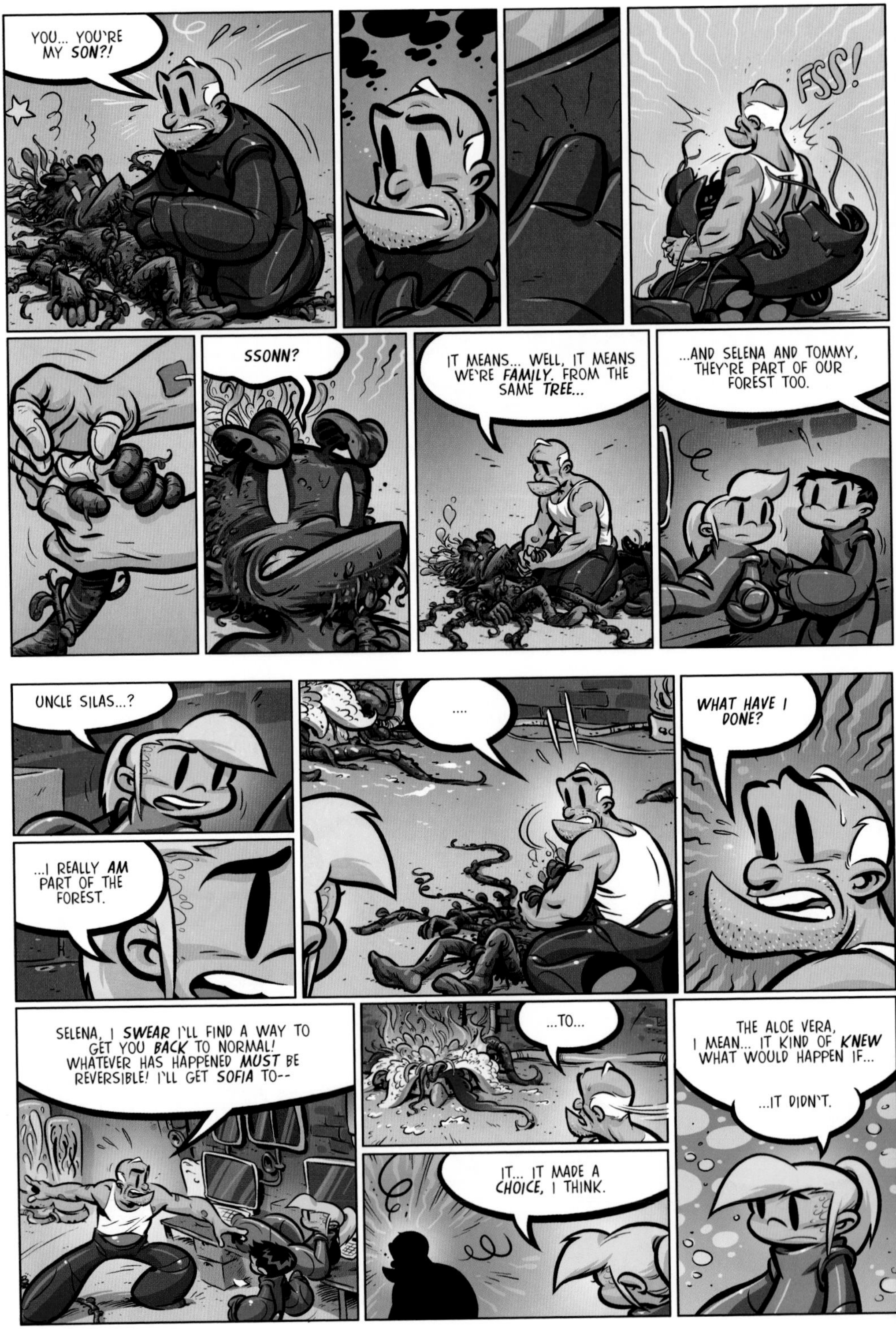
YOU... YOU'RE MY SON?!
FSS!
SSONN?
IT MEANS... WELL, IT MEANS WE'RE FAMILY. FROM THE SAME TREE...
...AND SELENA AND TOMMY, THEY'RE PART OF OUR FOREST TOO.
UNCLE SILAS...?
...I REALLY AM PART OF THE FOREST.
....
WHAT HAVE I DONE?
SELENA, I SWEAR I'LL FIND A WAY TO GET YOU BACK TO NORMAL! WHATEVER HAS HAPPENED MUST BE REVERSIBLE! I'LL GET SOFIA TO--
...TO...
IT... IT MADE A CHOICE, I THINK.
THE ALOE VERA, I MEAN... IT KIND OF KNEW WHAT WOULD HAPPEN IF...
...IT DIDN'T.

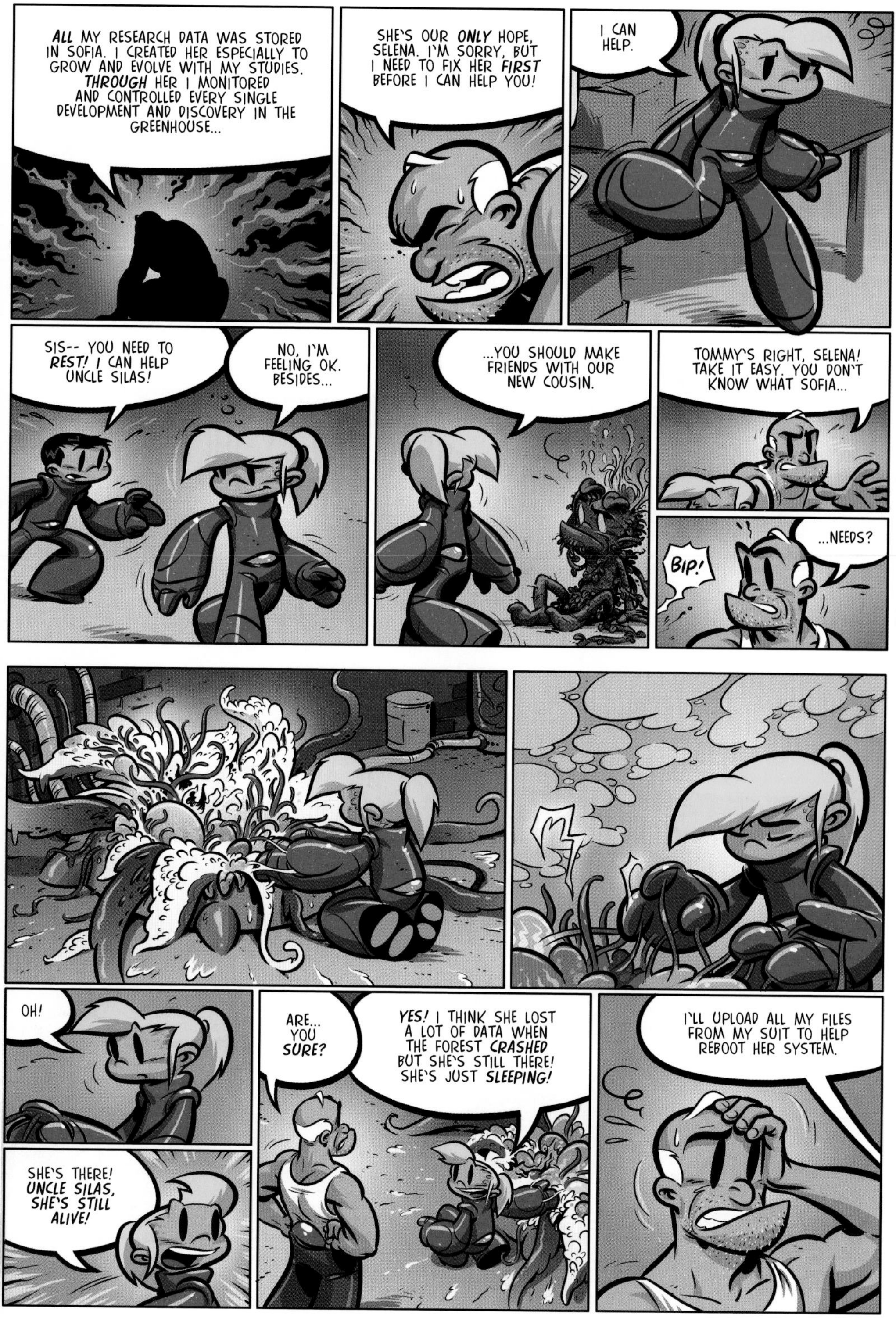
ALL MY RESEARCH DATA WAS STORED IN SOFIA. I CREATED HER ESPECIALLY TO GROW AND EVOLVE WITH MY STUDIES. THROUGH HER I MONITORED AND CONTROLLED EVERY SINGLE DEVELOPMENT AND DISCOVERY IN THE GREENHOUSE...
SHE'S OUR ONLY HOPE, SELENA. I'M SORRY, BUT I NEED TO FIX HER FIRST BEFORE I CAN HELP YOU!
I CAN HELP.
SIS-- YOU NEED TO REST! I CAN HELP UNCLE SILAS!
NO, I'M FEELING OK. BESIDES...
...YOU SHOULD MAKE FRIENDS WITH OUR NEW COUSIN.
TOMMY'S RIGHT, SELENA! TAKE IT EASY. YOU DON'T KNOW WHAT SOFIA...
BIP!
...NEEDS?
OH!
SHE'S THERE! UNCLE SILAS, SHE'S STILL ALIVE!
ARE... YOU SURE?
YES! I THINK SHE LOST A LOT OF DATA WHEN THE FOREST CRASHED BUT SHE'S STILL THERE! SHE'S JUST SLEEPING!
I'LL UPLOAD ALL MY FILES FROM MY SUIT TO HELP REBOOT HER SYSTEM.

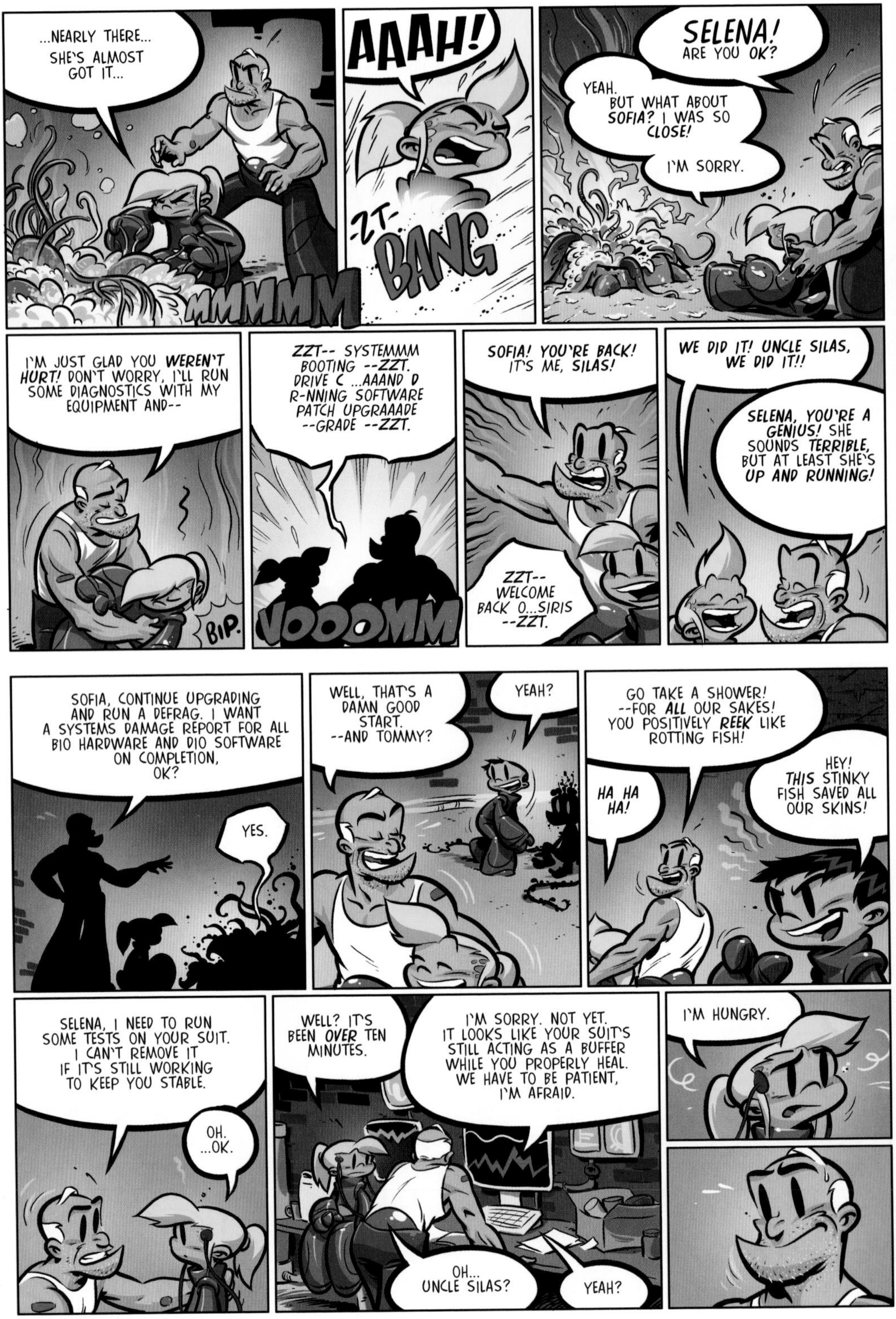
...NEARLY THERE... SHE'S ALMOST GOT IT...
MMMMMM
AAAH!
-ZT-
BANG
SELENA! ARE YOU OK?
YEAH. BUT WHAT ABOUT SOFIA? I WAS SO CLOSE!
I'M SORRY.
I'M JUST GLAD YOU WEREN'T HURT! DON'T WORRY, I'LL RUN SOME DIAGNOSTICS WITH MY EQUIPMENT AND--
BIP.
ZZT-- SYSTEMMM BOOTING --ZZT. DRIVE C ...AAAND D R-NNING SOFTWARE PATCH UPGRAAADE --GRADE --ZZT.
VOOOMM
SOFIA! YOU'RE BACK! IT'S ME, SILAS!
ZZT-- WELCOME BACK O...SIRIS --ZZT.
WE DID IT! UNCLE SILAS, WE DID IT!!
SELENA, YOU'RE A GENIUS! SHE SOUNDS TERRIBLE, BUT AT LEAST SHE'S UP AND RUNNING!
SOFIA, CONTINUE UPGRADING AND RUN A DEFRAG. I WANT A SYSTEMS DAMAGE REPORT FOR ALL BIO HARDWARE AND DIO SOFTWARE ON COMPLETION, OK?
YES.
WELL, THAT'S A DAMN GOOD START. --AND TOMMY?
YEAH?
GO TAKE A SHOWER! --FOR ALL OUR SAKES! YOU POSITIVELY REEK LIKE ROTTING FISH!
HA HA HA!
HEY! THIS STINKY FISH SAVED ALL OUR SKINS!
SELENA, I NEED TO RUN SOME TESTS ON YOUR SUIT. I CAN'T REMOVE IT IF IT'S STILL WORKING TO KEEP YOU STABLE.
OH. ...OK.
WELL? IT'S BEEN OVER TEN MINUTES.
I'M SORRY. NOT YET. IT LOOKS LIKE YOUR SUIT'S STILL ACTING AS A BUFFER WHILE YOU PROPERLY HEAL. WE HAVE TO BE PATIENT, I'M AFRAID.
OH... UNCLE SILAS?
YEAH?
I'M HUNGRY.

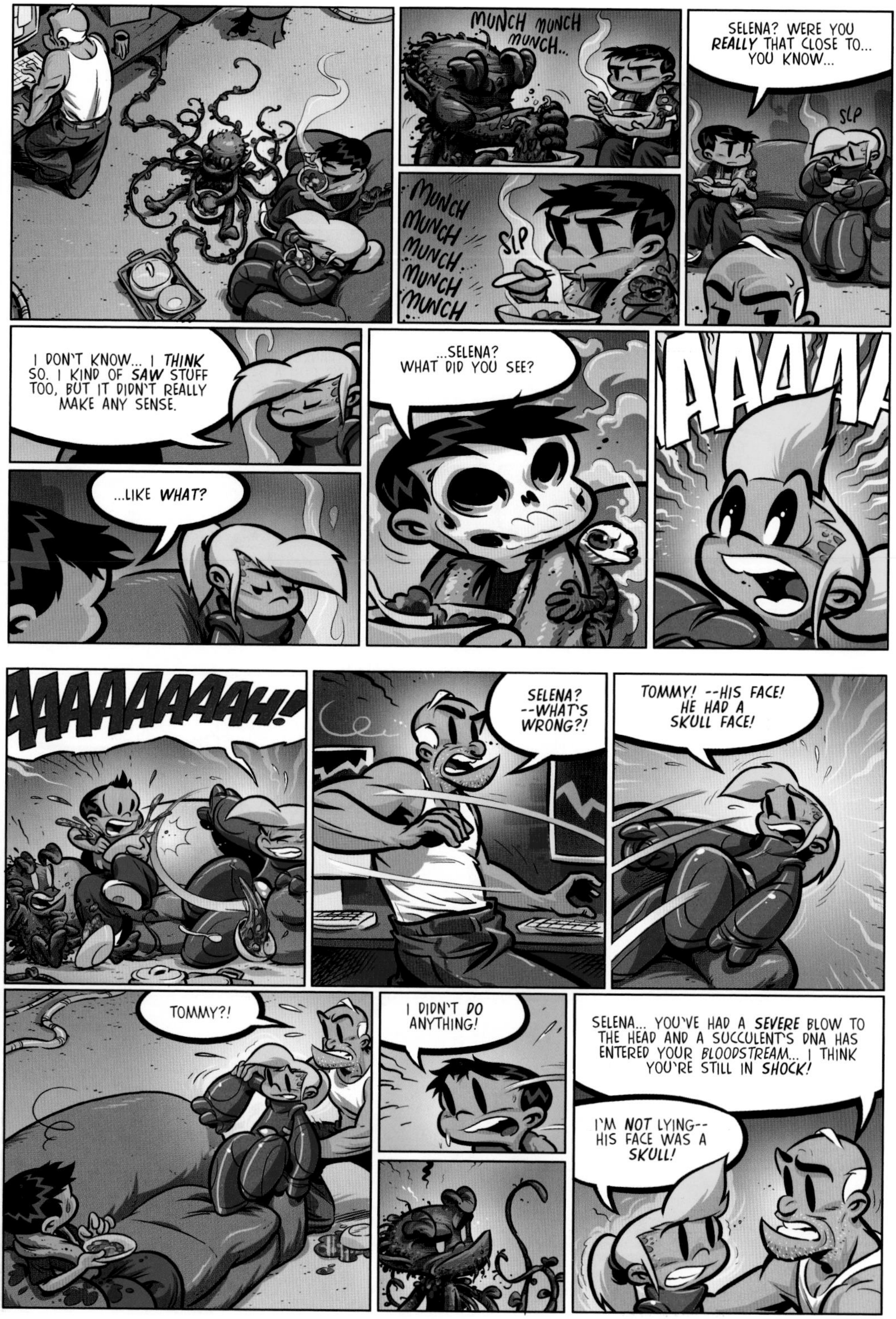
MUNCH MUNCH MUNCH...
SELENA? WERE YOU REALLY THAT CLOSE TO... YOU KNOW...
SLP
MUNCH MUNCH MUNCH MUNCH MUNCH
SLP
I DON'T KNOW... I THINK SO. I KIND OF SAW STUFF TOO, BUT IT DIDN'T REALLY MAKE ANY SENSE.
...LIKE WHAT?
...SELENA? WHAT DID YOU SEE?
AAAAAAAAAAAAAAH!
SELENA? --WHAT'S WRONG?!
TOMMY! --HIS FACE! HE HAD A SKULL FACE!
TOMMY?!
I DIDN'T DO ANYTHING!
SELENA... YOU'VE HAD A SEVERE BLOW TO THE HEAD AND A SUCCULENT'S DNA HAS ENTERED YOUR BLOODSTREAM... I THINK YOU'RE STILL IN SHOCK!
I'M NOT LYING-- HIS FACE WAS A SKULL!

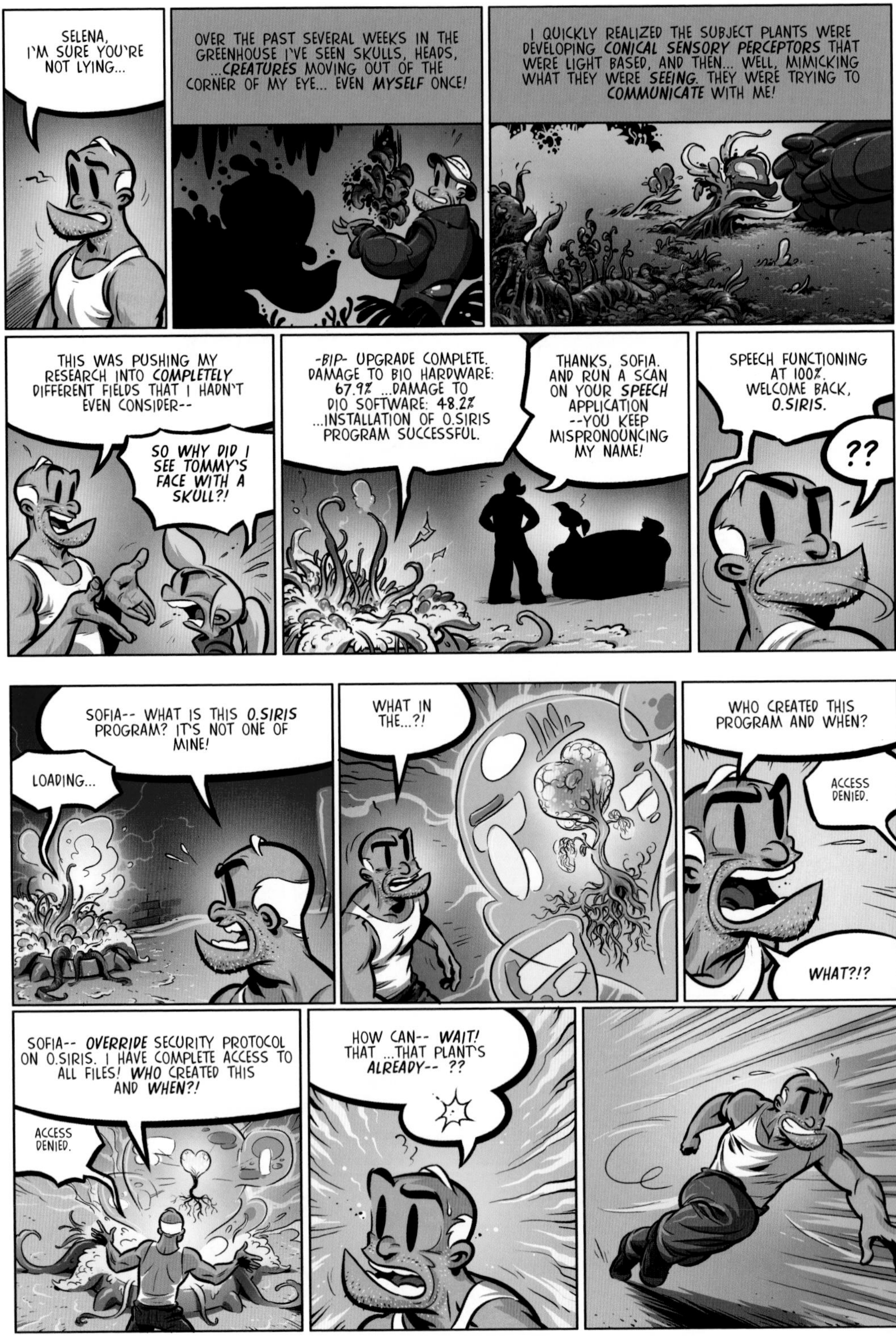
SELENA, I'M SURE YOU'RE NOT LYING...
OVER THE PAST SEVERAL WEEKS IN THE GREENHOUSE I'VE SEEN SKULLS, HEADS, ...CREATURES MOVING OUT OF THE CORNER OF MY EYE... EVEN MYSELF ONCE!
I QUICKLY REALIZED THE SUBJECT PLANTS WERE DEVELOPING CONICAL SENSORY PERCEPTORS THAT WERE LIGHT BASED, AND THEN... WELL, MIMICKING WHAT THEY WERE SEEING. THEY WERE TRYING TO COMMUNICATE WITH ME!
THIS WAS PUSHING MY RESEARCH INTO COMPLETELY DIFFERENT FIELDS THAT I HADN'T EVEN CONSIDER--
SO WHY DID I SEE TOMMY'S FACE WITH A SKULL?!
-BIP- UPGRADE COMPLETE. DAMAGE TO BIO HARDWARE: 67.9% ...DAMAGE TO BIO SOFTWARE: 48.2% ...INSTALLATION OF O.SIRIS PROGRAM SUCCESSFUL.
THANKS, SOFIA. AND RUN A SCAN ON YOUR SPEECH APPLICATION --YOU KEEP MISPRONOUNCING MY NAME!
SPEECH FUNCTIONING AT 100%. WELCOME BACK, O.SIRIS.
??
SOFIA-- WHAT IS THIS O.SIRIS PROGRAM? IT'S NOT ONE OF MINE!
LOADING...
WHAT IN THE...?!
WHO CREATED THIS PROGRAM AND WHEN?
ACCESS DENIED.
WHAT?!?
SOFIA-- OVERRIDE SECURITY PROTOCOL ON O.SIRIS. I HAVE COMPLETE ACCESS TO ALL FILES! WHO CREATED THIS AND WHEN?!
ACCESS DENIED.
HOW CAN-- WAIT! THAT ...THAT PLANT'S ALREADY-- ??

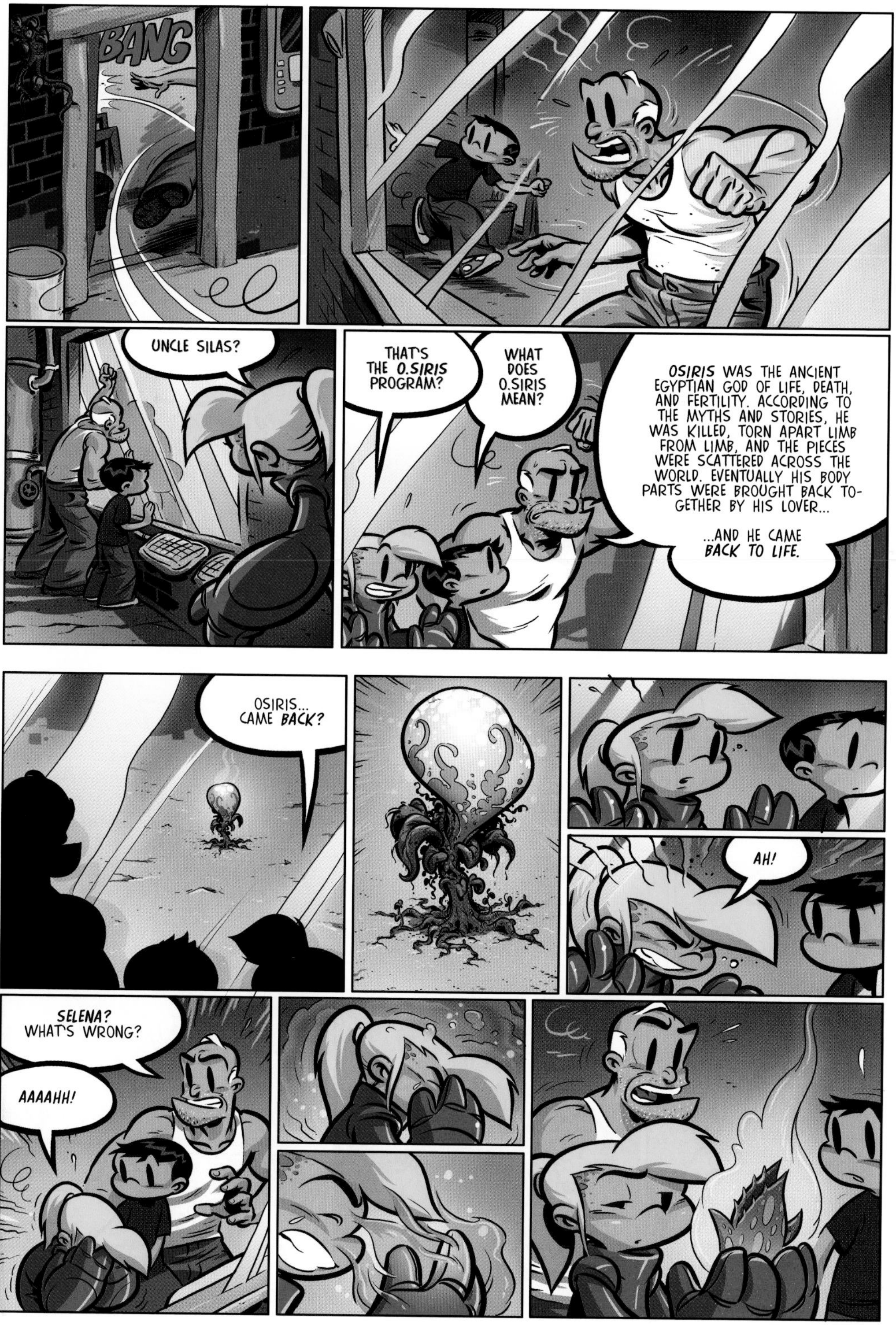
BANG
UNCLE SILAS?
THAT'S THE O.SIRIS PROGRAM?
WHAT DOES O.SIRIS MEAN?
OSIRIS WAS THE ANCIENT EGYPTIAN GOD OF LIFE, DEATH, AND FERTILITY. ACCORDING TO THE MYTHS AND STORIES, HE WAS KILLED, TORN APART LIMB FROM LIMB, AND THE PIECES WERE SCATTERED ACROSS THE WORLD. EVENTUALLY HIS BODY PARTS WERE BROUGHT BACK TO-GETHER BY HIS LOVER...
...AND HE CAME BACK TO LIFE.
OSIRIS... CAME BACK?
AH!
SELENA? WHAT'S WRONG?
AAAAHH!

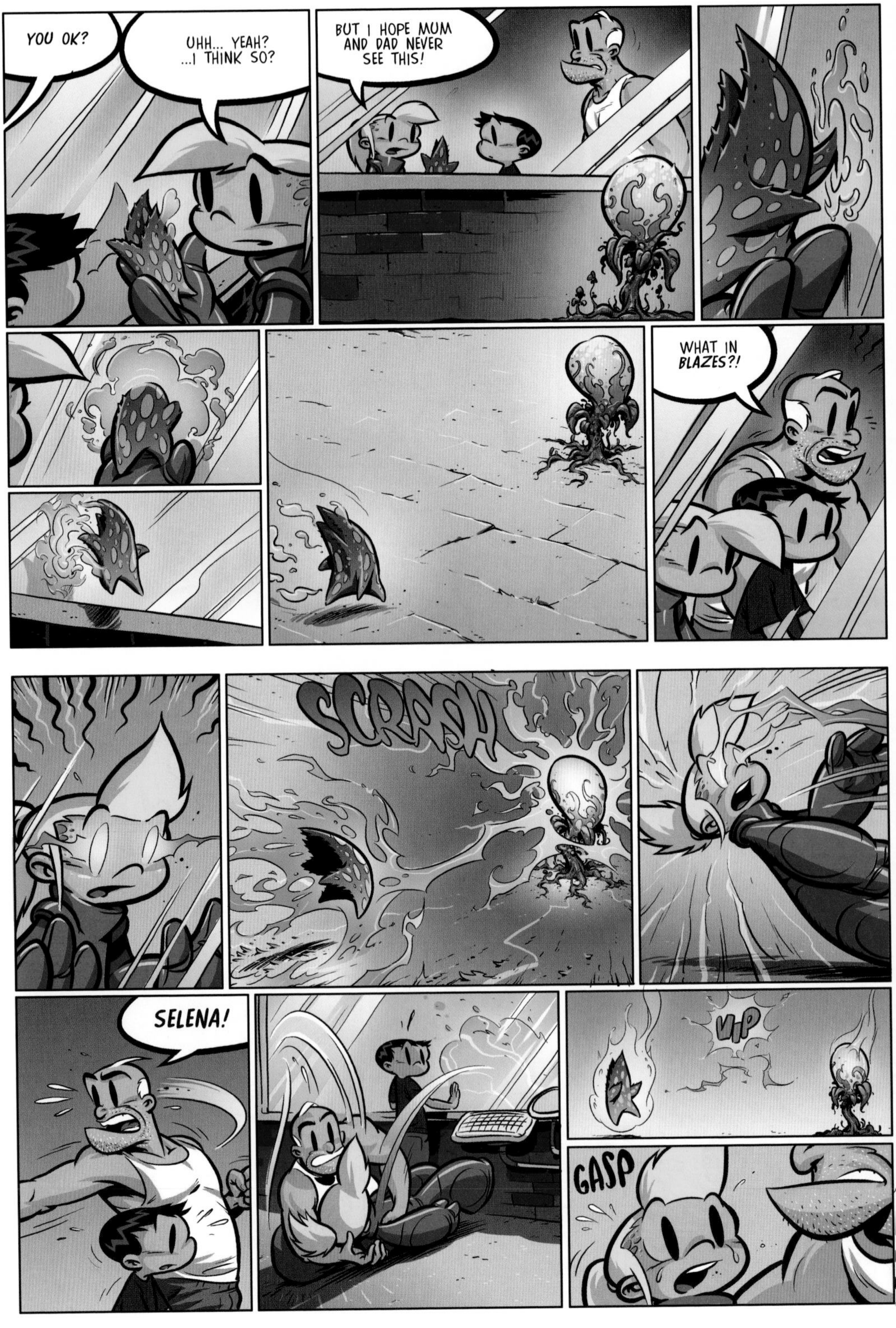
YOU OK?
UHH... YEAH? ...I THINK SO?
BUT I HOPE MUM AND DAD NEVER SEE THIS!
WHAT IN BLAZES?!
SCRASH
SELENA!
VIP
GASP

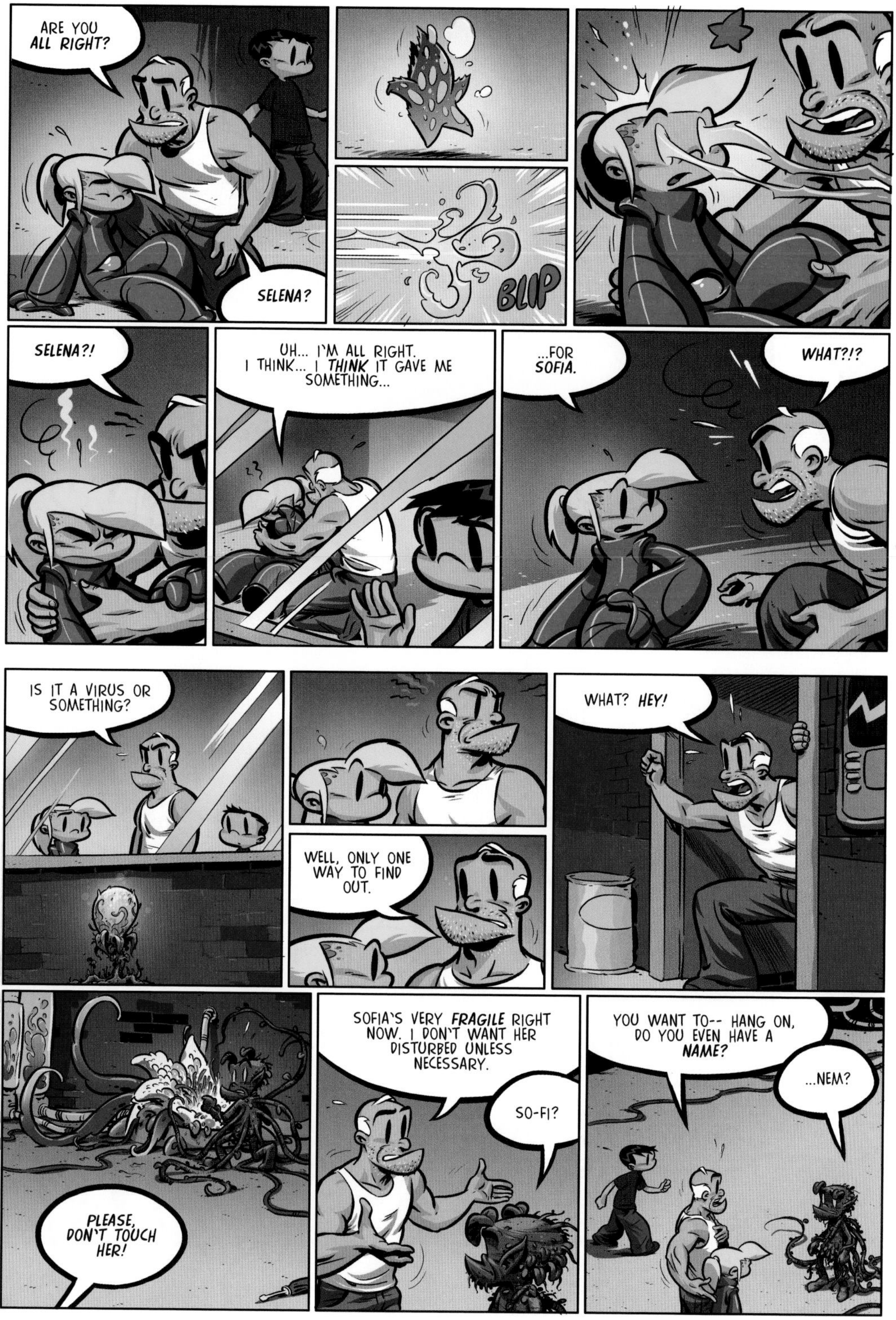
ARE YOU ALL RIGHT?
SELENA?
BLIP
SELENA?!
UH... I'M ALL RIGHT. I THINK... I THINK IT GAVE ME SOMETHING...
...FOR SOFIA.
WHAT?!?
IS IT A VIRUS OR SOMETHING?
WELL, ONLY ONE WAY TO FIND OUT.
WHAT? HEY!
PLEASE, DON'T TOUCH HER!
SOFIA'S VERY FRAGILE RIGHT NOW. I DON'T WANT HER DISTURBED UNLESS NECESSARY.
SO-FI?
YOU WANT TO-- HANG ON, DO YOU EVEN HAVE A NAME?
...NEM?

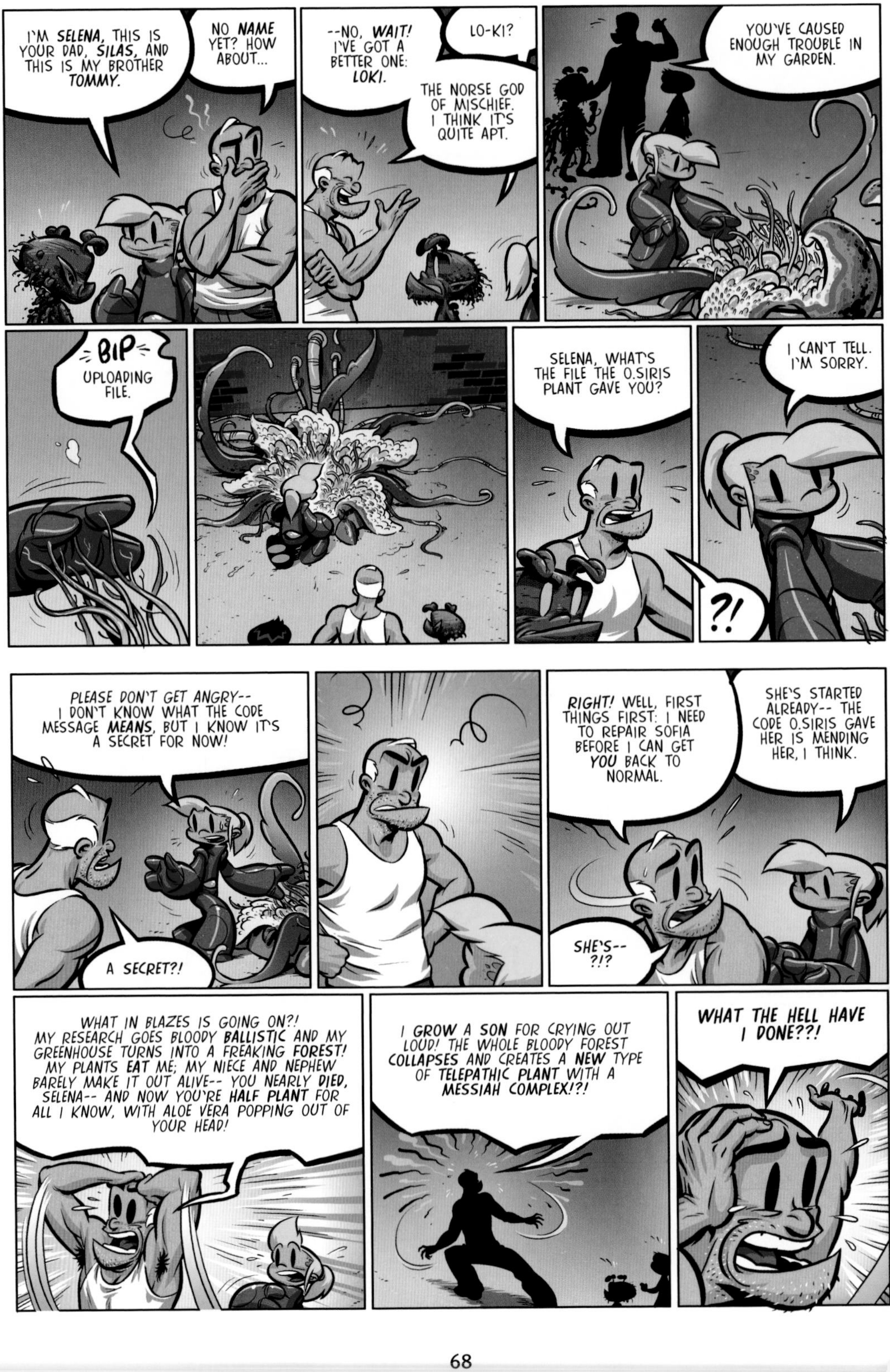
I'M SELENA, THIS IS YOUR DAD, SILAS, AND THIS IS MY BROTHER TOMMY.
NO NAME YET? HOW ABOUT...
--NO, WAIT! I'VE GOT A BETTER ONE: LOKI.
LO-KI?
THE NORSE GOD OF MISCHIEF. I THINK IT'S QUITE APT.
YOU'VE CAUSED ENOUGH TROUBLE IN MY GARDEN.
BIP
UPLOADING FILE.
SELENA, WHAT'S THE FILE THE O.SIRIS PLANT GAVE YOU?
?!
I CAN'T TELL. I'M SORRY.
PLEASE DON'T GET ANGRY-- I DON'T KNOW WHAT THE CODE MESSAGE MEANS, BUT I KNOW IT'S A SECRET FOR NOW!
A SECRET?!
RIGHT! WELL, FIRST THINGS FIRST: I NEED TO REPAIR SOFIA BEFORE I CAN GET YOU BACK TO NORMAL.
SHE'S STARTED ALREADY-- THE CODE O.SIRIS GAVE HER IS MENDING HER, I THINK.
SHE'S-- ?!?
WHAT IN BLAZES IS GOING ON?! MY RESEARCH GOES BLOODY BALLISTIC AND MY GREENHOUSE TURNS INTO A FREAKING FOREST! MY PLANTS EAT ME; MY NIECE AND NEPHEW BARELY MAKE IT OUT ALIVE-- YOU NEARLY DIED, SELENA-- AND NOW YOU'RE HALF PLANT FOR ALL I KNOW, WITH ALOE VERA POPPING OUT OF YOUR HEAD!
I GROW A SON FOR CRYING OUT LOUD! THE WHOLE BLOODY FOREST COLLAPSES AND CREATES A NEW TYPE OF TELEPATHIC PLANT WITH A MESSIAH COMPLEX!?!
WHAT THE HELL HAVE I DONE??!

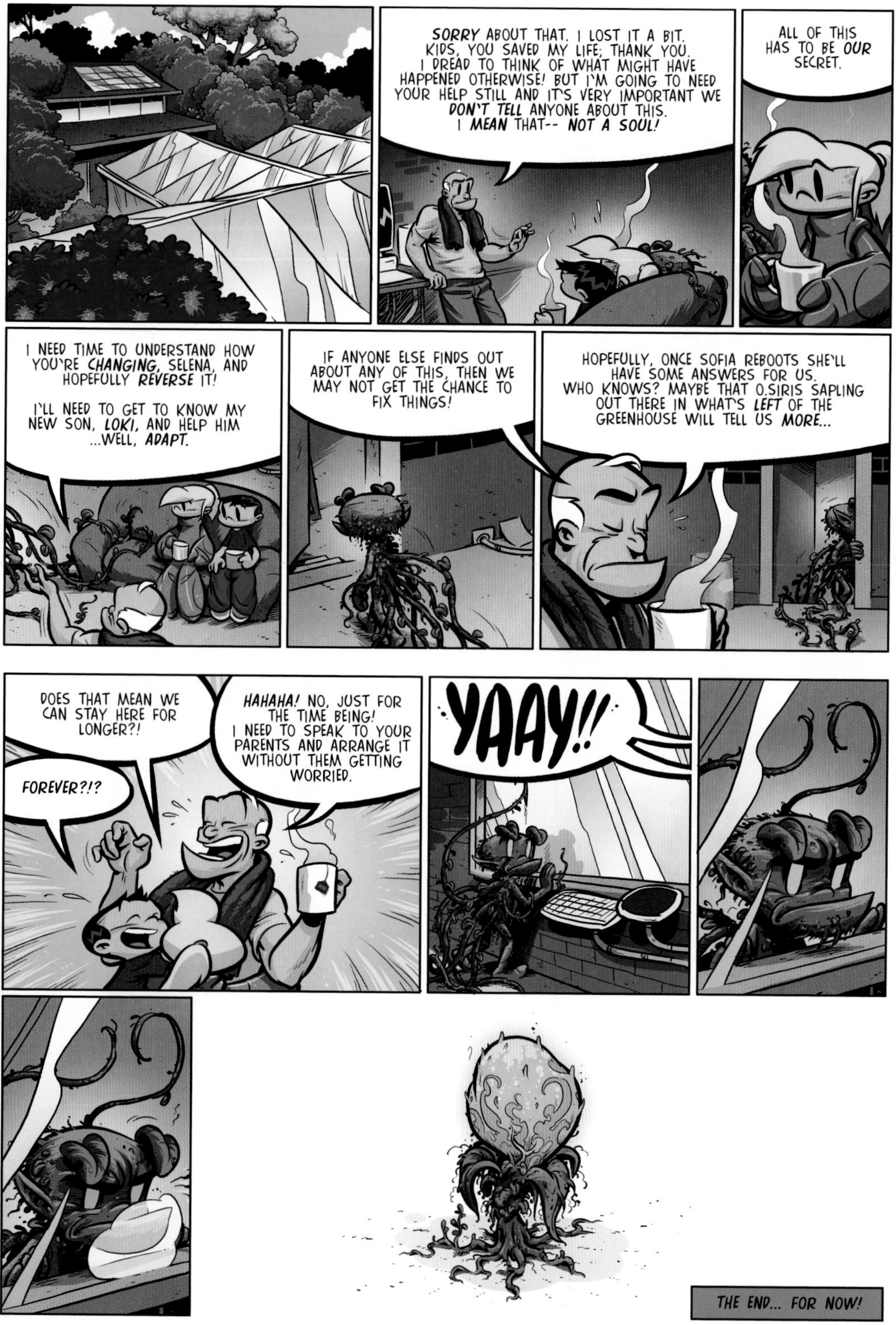
SORRY ABOUT THAT. I LOST IT A BIT. KIDS, YOU SAVED MY LIFE; THANK YOU. I DREAD TO THINK OF WHAT MIGHT HAVE HAPPENED OTHERWISE! BUT I'M GOING TO NEED YOUR HELP STILL AND IT'S VERY IMPORTANT WE DON'T TELL ANYONE ABOUT THIS. I MEAN THAT-- NOT A SOUL!
ALL OF THIS HAS TO BE OUR SECRET.
I NEED TIME TO UNDERSTAND HOW YOU'RE CHANGING, SELENA, AND HOPEFULLY REVERSE IT!
I'LL NEED TO GET TO KNOW MY NEW SON, LOKI, AND HELP HIM ...WELL, ADAPT.
IF ANYONE ELSE FINDS OUT ABOUT ANY OF THIS, THEN WE MAY NOT GET THE CHANCE TO FIX THINGS!
HOPEFULLY, ONCE SOFIA REBOOTS SHE'LL HAVE SOME ANSWERS FOR US. WHO KNOWS? MAYBE THAT O.SIRIS SAPLING OUT THERE IN WHAT'S LEFT OF THE GREENHOUSE WILL TELL US MORE...
DOES THAT MEAN WE CAN STAY HERE FOR LONGER?!
FOREVER?!?
HAHAHA! NO, JUST FOR THE TIME BEING! I NEED TO SPEAK TO YOUR PARENTS AND ARRANGE IT WITHOUT THEM GETTING WORRIED.
YAAY!!
THE END... FOR NOW!

MORE COOL STUFF TO READ FROM DARK HORSE BOOKS!

STAR WARS: THE CLONE WARS—
IN SERVICE OF THE REPUBLIC
Written by Henry Gilroy and Steven Melching
Art by Scott Hepburn, Dan Parsons,
and Ramón Pérez

Jedi Kit Fisto and Plo Koon take on a daring assault mission with a squad of tough Republic commandos on the ice planet Khorm. The Jedi seek to free the Separatist-enslaved Khormai people and destroy the Separatists' mountain fortress. But on this assignment, nothing will come easy!

ISBN 978-1-59582-487-5 $7.99

GIANT SIZE LITTLE LULU VOLUME 1
Written by John Stanley
Art by John Stanley and Irving Tripp

Lulu Moppet is the true-blue daughter of Main Street America, an eight-year-old hero for anyone who ever wanted to bring home a gorilla, scare the pants off of ghosts, and outwit every grownup in sight. Collecting some of the earliest, out-of-print volumes of Dark Horse's acclaimed reprint series, this massive 664-page omnibus is the most affordable way to build a library of John Stanley's masterpiece!

ISBN 978-1-59582-502-5 $24.99

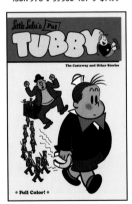

LITTLE LULU'S PAL TUBBY
VOLUME 1: THE CASTAWAY AND OTHER STORIES
Stories and Art by John Stanley

The comedic genius of John Stanley couldn't be contained by one series alone; in 1952 Lulu's pal Tubby made his solo debut in his own hysterical comic. Filled with all the charm and hilarity of *Little Lulu*, *Tubby* is a familiar but different delight from comics legend John Stanley! Dark Horse is proud to present these never-before-reprinted gems from comics' golden age in a new series of full-color paperback collections.

ISBN 978-1-59582-421-9 $15.99

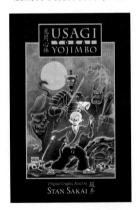

USAGI YOJIMBO: YOKAI
Story and Art by Stan Sakai

The rabbit ronin turns twenty-five, and Dark Horse celebrates with the first-ever *Usagi Yojimbo* original graphic novel, fully hand-painted, written, and lettered by creator Stan Sakai! *Yokai* are the monsters, demons, and spirits of Japanese folklore. Usagi faces these unpredictable supernatural creatures when a desperate woman begs for his help in finding her kidnapped daughter.

ISBN 978-1-59582-362-5 $14.99

DARK HORSE BOOKS®
darkhorse.com

BRODY'S GHOST
MARK CRILLEY
RIP

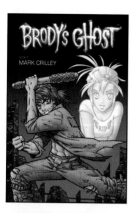

BRODY'S GHOST BOOK 1

Story and Art by Mark Crilley

Thirteen-time Eisner nominee Mark Crilley joins Dark Horse to launch his most original and action-packed saga to date in *Brody's Ghost*. Brody comes face to face with a ghostly teenaged girl who tells him she needs his help in hunting down a dangerous killer, and that he must undergo training from the spirit of a centuries-old samurai to unlock his hidden supernatural powers.

ISBN 978-1-59582-521-6 $6.99

HARVEY COMICS CLASSICS VOLUME FIVE
The
HARVEY GIRLS
LITTLE AUDREY, LITTLE DOT & LITTLE LOTTA
125
Classic
Comic
Stories
1949–1966
Edited by LESLIE CABARGA
Introduction by JERRY BECK

HARVEY COMICS CLASSICS

VOLUME FIVE: THE HARVEY GIRLS

Edited by Leslie Cabarga

Introduction by Jerry Beck

They're cute, they're clever, and they're obsessive! Some of Harvey Comics' biggest stars were three "little" girls with large dreams, enormous hearts, and king-size laughs: Little Audrey, Little Dot, and Little Lotta. Featuring an introduction from comics expert Jerry Beck, *Harvey Girls* just want to have fun!

ISBN 978-1-59582-171-3 $19.99

SHADOW ROCK
JEREMY LOVE and ROBERT LOVE

SHADOW ROCK

Written by Jeremy Love

Art by Robert Love and Jeremy Love

Harrowing thrills and chills ensue in this classic boys' adventure with a horror twist! After his mother's death, young Timothy London moves from the big city to the small New England fishing town of Shadow Rock. Timothy and his new ghostly companion Kendahl set out to explore the dark underbelly of Shadow Rock and the mystery of Kendahl's death.

ISBN 978-1-59307-347-3 $9.99

GEAR SCHOOL
GALLARDO • PERIS • SANDOVAL

GEAR SCHOOL

Written by Adam Gallardo

Art by Núria Peris and Sergio Sandoval

Thirteen-year-old Teresa Gottlieb has just entered a prestigious military academy, known to all as Gear School, to try to become one of its elite students. But on top of all the usual troubles that a seventh grader has to put up with—boys, social cliques, hellish instructors—she also has to deal with three-story-tall robots and alien invasions!

ISBN 978-1-59307-854-6 $7.99

AVAILABLE AT YOUR LOCAL COMICS SHOP OR BOOKSTORE!

To find a comics shop in your area, call 1-888-266-4226.

For more information or to order direct, visit darkhorse.com or call 1-800-862-0052 Mon.–Fri. 9 AM to 5 PM Pacific Time.